Themes in the Gospel of John

Dr. Randy Colver

Themes in the Gospel of John
Copyright © 2009 by Dr. Randy Colver
All rights reserved.
Revised March 2016.

ISBN 978-0-615-36214-4

Scripture taken from the HOLY BIBLE,
NEW INTERNATIONAL VERSION®.
NIV®. Copyright © 1973, 1978, 1984, by International Bible Society.
Used by permission of Zondervan Publishing House. All rights reserved.

Contents

Introduction 5

1. John's Purpose and Major Theme 7
2. The Father and Son Relationship Theme 13
3. The Trial Theme 21
4. The Conflict Theme (Belief and Unbelief) 31
5. Old Testament Themes in John's Prologue 39
6. The Theme of the Holy Spirit 45
7. The Theme of Love 53
8. The Theme of Glory 61
9. The Theme of Life 69
10. Themes in the Nicodemus Discourse 77
11. Themes in the Samaritan Woman Discourse 81
12. Themes in the Man Born Blind Discourse 87
A. Locating the Belief/Unbelief Conflict 93
B. Belief/Unbelief Conflict in John's Gospel 95
C. The Structure of John's Gospel 97
D. Christ as the Faithful and True Witness 101

Introduction

Purpose of this Class

Rather than spend a great deal of time examining the reliability, date of the gospel, outline, and other background information (which is provided by many quality commentaries), this class will concentrate on important themes in John's gospel. Our purpose is to accept the book as it is and explore the themes (theology) John weaves through his book. (We will touch on some background information when it underscores a theme.)

A theme is a subject of importance that is repeated and developed throughout a book. Gary Burge quoted C. H. Dodd as describing the Gospel of John like a musical fugue:

> A theme is introduced and developed up to a point; then a second theme is introduced and the two are interwoven; then a third and so on. A theme may be dropped, and later resumed and differently combined, in all manner of harmonious variations.[1]

These themes not only help us understand the overall message of the Gospel of John, but each theme also reveals some aspect of the Person of Christ (Christology). Ultimately, John's desire was to bring the reader to saving faith in the Lord Jesus Christ.

John declared, "Now this is eternal life: that they may know you, the only true God, and Jesus Christ, whom you have sent" (Jn. 17:3). Eternal life is not just a theological concept, or a belief in the after-life. Eternal life is wrapped up from beginning to end in the Person of Christ. Neither is eternal life an academic knowledge of Jesus. It is a deep, inner work of revelation and change. The Father has sent His Son to reveal God to man. Christ is *the representative* of the Father. He is the only way to the Father, and hence, to eternal life.

To this same end, the purpose of this class is to know Christ. Each theme that John has woven into the fabric of his book will help us know our Lord more completely.

Lesson Layout

Each lesson will cover a theme in John's Gospel. However, rather than simply lecture on a theme, you will have the opportunity to discover the theme. Key verses will be listed for the class to examine and make comments. After developing the theme, you will then have the opportunity to apply the theme to your life. Application is vitally important. We cannot hold spiritual things "from the outside." We must make them real to us on the inside. Gary Burge noted:

> George MacDonald once said that nothing is so deadening to the Divine as to habitually deal with the *outside* of holy things...C. S. Lewis, in his autobiography, *Surprised by Joy*, put it this way: "The problem of the pastorate is that those who hold holy things too often soon become callous to the feel of their touch."[2]

The point is well taken, and bears constant recall. Application of the truths of the gospel is John's purpose in every respect: "That believing they may have *life* in His name." Life comes when truth is applied.

As you read through the Gospel of John, record Scripture references for each of the major themes. This will help you to understand each theme as we discuss them in class.

After examining the key themes, we will explore them further in three major discourses. These constitute the last three lessons. The appendixes add a few important thoughts about the conflict between belief and unbelief in John's Gospel, and some insights about the structure of the Gospel itself.

1

John's Purpose and Major Theme

Bible Review

Read through the following verses. Pay careful attention to the deity of Christ and John's purpose for writing His Gospel.

Key Scriptures

John 1:1
Key Thought _____

_____

John 1:18
Key Thought _____

_____

John 8:57-59
Key Thought _____

_____

John 10:27-33
Key Thought _____

_____

John 20:27-28
Key Thought _____

_____

John 20:30-31
Key Thought _____

_____

Themes in the Gospel of John

Answer the following questions related to your Bible study.

Comments and Analysis

1. Does John reveal the purpose for writing his gospel? What is that purpose?

2. If John is successful in his purpose, what would be the result?

3. Does John reveal part of his method to accomplish the desired results?

4. What is an apologetic work? Should John's book be used in evangelism? Why or why not?

5. Who is the Word? Is the Word deity? Who does Jesus claim to be? Did the Jews recognize Jesus' claim to be God? What did they consider it to be?

6. Did Jesus accept or reject Thomas' pronouncement?

7. Is Thomas like the reader who comes to the revelation of who Christ is? Is this possibly the climax of John's Gospel?

Review of John's Purpose and Major Theme

As we noted before, the overarching theme of John's gospel is plainly stated in Chapter 20:30-31:

> Jesus did many other miraculous signs in the presence of his disciples, which are not recorded in this book. But these are written that you may believe that Jesus is the Christ, the Son of God, and that by believing you may have life in his name.

In expounding one of the most important themes in John's gospel, Beasley-Murray emphasizes the latter half of this verse: *that by believing you may have life in his name.* John's gospel is the Gospel of Life.[1] Christ brought life through His kingdom. In support of this, Beasley-Murray notes John 5:24:

> "I tell you the truth, whoever hears my word and believes him who sent me has eternal life and will not be condemned; he has crossed over from death to life" (see further 3:36; 4:14; 6:47, 53; 17:3).

This life is found in Christ (Jn. 1:4; 5:26; 6:40, 68; 10:10), and in Him only (Jn. 14:6). Although "life" is a significant theme in John's gospel, it is only part of John's purpose. John 20:30-31 lists life as the result of believing. The first step is to bring the reader into saving faith. Therefore, faith is a predominant theme as well.[2]

This brings us to the method that John wishes to bring the reader into faith: "*These are written that you may believe...*" John's gospel is apologetic in nature. He wishes to give evidence that life can be found in Christ. John selects those events in Christ's life that are necessary to bring the reader into saving faith.

Finally, we must believe that "Jesus *is* the Christ, the Son of God." It is not enough to believe that Christ provides some means among many to obtain "life," no matter how abundant. It is necessary to believe that Christ *is* God. For that is the whole summary of John's prologue: "No one has ever seen God, but God the One and Only, who is at the Father's side, has made him known" (John 1:18). How has the Father made God, the "Unique One," known? That is what John shows us in his gospel.

Unless Christ is God, there can be no life given in His name. If Christ was nothing more than an exalted creation of God, then He needs a Redeemer Himself, for "the creation was subjected to frustration" (Ro. 8:20). This is all too well understood by the Evangelist. Unless he can demonstrate that Jesus is who He said He was, then the purpose fails. When John claims that Christ is the "resurrection and the life," he is not just making a statement about life, he is demonstrating to the world that Christ *is* Life by the raising of Lazarus from the dead.

Keep in mind that the themes in John's Gospel are often double-edged and may point to several important themes at one time.[3] Nevertheless, each theme supports John's apologetic purpose. Like a weaver/author, John drew out of his theological "sewing box" the illustrations of Christ's life and sewed them skillfully together like patches in a quilt. Together they make a spiritual "comforter" that can wrap us up in God's love.

---

[1] See also Jn. 3:15, 36; 5:27; 6:47, 58; 11:25-26.
[2] The word faith is used over 98 times in John's Gospel. The struggle between belief and unbelief is a primary motif.
[3] Even the words can have more than one meaning. For instance, "born again" can also mean "born from above" (Jn. 3:3,7).

John's purpose forms a framework for interpreting his gospel. The various parts of the gospel, including the prologue, events, discourses, movements between narratives, and the explanatory notes of John,[4] all work together to support John's theme. John is no different than the Synoptic authors in presenting the historical account of Jesus along with their unique purpose and perspective. "Each Evangelist presents theology along with history and 'interprets' Jesus for readers."[5] John takes from his own resources those pieces of Christ's life that are necessary to prove his theme. These are sewn together to prove His deity and bring the reader to Life in Christ.

The Deity of Christ in John's Gospel

If Christ is the Son of God, then He is deity. John records the following: "For this cause therefore the Jews were seeking all the more to kill Him, because He not only was breaking the Sabbath, but also was calling God His own Father, *making Himself equal with God*" (Jn. 5:18). The Jews clearly understood Christ's claims.

The deity of Christ is established in the Prologue and developed through John's book. Let's look at the deity of Christ in the Prologue a little closer.

Jn. 1:1

- "In the beginning was the Word..." This means that the Word is pre-existent. He was not "after" or "from" or created. He was *in* the beginning.

- "The Word was with God..." The word "with" is not the usual Greek word for "next to" or "alongside" (meta), but rather one that means "toward" (pros) and suggests a "face-to-face" relationship of equals.[6]

- "The Word was God..." John flatly states that the Word is God (theos). He is co-equal with the Father, of whom He enjoys an intimate relationship. Some have tried to say that this means that Christ is "divine" in some way less than God. D. A. Carson retorts, "This will not do. There is a perfectly serviceable word in Greek for 'divine' (namely *theios*)."[7]

Jn. 1:3 - Christ is the Creator of all things. This means that He Himself is uncreated.[8]

Jn. 1:14 - "The Word was made flesh..." This verse identifies Jesus as the Word and declares that God has become incarnate.

Jn. 1:18 - "The unique God, who is at the Father's side, has made Him known." John again clearly declares Christ to be God and portrays Him as having an intimate relationship with the Father as an equal.

---

[4] The explanatory notes are what Merrill C. Tenney called, "the footnotes" in John's gospel. See Merrill C. Tenney, *The Footnotes of John's Gospel*, Bibliotheca Sacra, Oct. 1960, 350-363.
[5] Gary M. Burge, *Interpreting the Gospel of John* (Grand Rapids: Baker Book House, 1992), 26.
[6] A. T. Robertson, *The Divinity of Christ in the Gospel of John*, 39.
[7] D. A. Carson, *The Gospel According to John* (Grand Rapids: William. B. Eerdmans Publishing Co., 1991), 117.
[8] Robertson noted that the emphasis in the Greek was that not only all things were made by Him, but "every single thing." Op. cit., 40. See also Rev. 3:14.

Besides the Prologue, the following Scriptures specifically reveal the deity of Christ in John's gospel:

- Jn. 5:18 - The Pharisees recognized that Jesus was making himself equal with God.

- Jn. 5:22-23 - Honor the Son just as you honor the Father.

- Jn. 8:58 - Jesus identifies Himself as the eternal "I Am." (See Ex. 3:14 and Is. 41:4.)

- Jn. 10:28-30 - Jesus expressed the absolute unity of Himself with the Father.

- Jn. 17:5 - Jesus shares the glory of the Father.

- Jn. 20:28 - Thomas calls Jesus both Lord and God.[9]

Christ's miracles and resurrection also substantiate His deity. He had power over life and death. Christ's deity is therefore a major theme in John's Gospel.[10] It provides the foundation for what John wants to reveal to us about Christ. Does John do a convincing job? We will see in the next two lessons.

Summary

Norman Geisler summarized the overall apologetic argument of John's Gospel:[11]

1. "The theistic God exists;
2. In a theistic universe, miracles are possible;
3. Miracles in connection with truth claims are acts of God that confirm the truth of God claimed by a messenger of God;
4. The New Testament documents are historically reliable;
5. In the New Testament Jesus claimed to be God;
6. Jesus proved to be God by unprecedented convergence of miracles;
7. Therefore, Jesus was God in human flesh."

John gives us a brilliant portrait of Christ in his gospel. He is the Son of God. Deity has taken on flesh and tabernacled among men. The theme of Christ's deity, therefore, is the essence of the gospel. It is at the core of Christianity—the fundamental belief necessary to obtain life in the kingdom of God. Only eternal God can give eternal life. This is the central concept of which John wrote: "Whoever believes in Him will not perish but have eternal life" (Jn. 3:16).

---

[9] This is the climax of the gospel. Note that Jesus did not correct him, but received what he said.

[10] The other gospels also record several of Christ's claims to deity: Mt. 16:16-17, 28:9; Mk. 2:5-10, 5:6, 14:61-65, 15:19. Since Luke stressed the humanity of Christ, it should not be surprising that the other gospels have more to say about Christ's deity.

[11] Norman Geisler, *The Apologetic Importance of John's Gospel*, 1. Paper delivered to the Southeastern Regional Meeting of the Evangelical Theological Society, March, 1996.

Application

1. If Christ is not God, is salvation possible? Explain.

2. Comment on the following: "Jesus is fully God and fully human."

3. Comment on Jesus' self-esteem from Jn. 13:3-5.

4. In light of John's overall theme, what does the following statement mean to you? "God has invaded history."

5. How should we respond to the knowledge that God became incarnate to suffer and die so that we might have life?

2

The Father and Son Relationship Theme

Bible Review

Read through the following verses from John's Gospel. Pay careful attention to the many aspects of the Father and Son relationship.

Key Scriptures

John 2:16-17
Key Thought _____
_____

John 3:35
Key Thought _____
_____

John 5:20-23
Key Thought _____
_____

John 6:27
Key Thought _____
_____

John 7:28-29
Key Thought _____
_____

John 8:16
Key Thought _____
_____

John 14:6-11a
Key Thought _____
_____

Comments and Analysis

1. How well did Christ know the Father? How was Christ zealous for the Father's things?

2. What authority did the Father give the Son? Who sent the Son? What does that mean?

3. How did Christ reveal the Father?

4. Was Christ confident of His purpose? Was He confident of His Father's approval and support (Jn. 3:35; 6:27; 8:16)?

5. If knowing Christ means knowing the Father, what does Christ's life reveal about the Father?

6. Describe the kind of Father/Son relationship expressed in these verses.

Review of the Father/Son Relationship Theme

Intimate Relationship

The Father and the Son in close, co-equal relationship is an important theme in the Fourth Gospel. Several Scriptures are given below to illustrate this:

- Jn. 5:17-18 - As the Father worked, so the Son worked.

- Jn. 5:21-23, 26 - As the Father raises the dead and gives them life, so the Son gives life.

- Jn. 7:16-17 - The words that the Father gives, the Son gives to others.

- Jn. 8:28, 38; 12:49-50 - The Son speaks the things He sees the Father doing.

- Jn. 10:15 - As the Father knows the Son, so the Son knows the Father.

- Jn. 14:9 - If you have seen the Son, you have seen the Father.

- Jn. 15:18-19, 23 - To not honor the Son is to not honor the Father.

- Jn. 16:15, 17:10 - All that belongs to the Father belongs also to the Son.

The Father/Son Relationship and the Deity of Christ

Closely related to and supporting the deity of Christ is the important theme of the Father and Son relationship. More than any other gospel writer, John records the intimate, loving, and unified relationship between the first and second Persons of the Trinity. D.A. Carson writes:

> Although "Son of God" can serve as a rough synonym for "Messiah," it is enriched by the unique manner in which Jesus as God's Son relates to his Father. He is functionally subordinate to him, and does only those things that the Father gives him to say and do, but he does *everything* that the Father does, since the Father shows him everything that he himself does. The perfection of Jesus' obedience and the unqualified nature of his dependence thereby become the loci in which Jesus discloses nothing less than the words and deeds of God.[12]

Gary Burge affirms:

> It is the Father himself who is present in Jesus (hence John's full divinity of Jesus) and this validates both his words and works...But here we must recall Jesus' consistent subordination to his Father's will (5:19, 30; 6:38; 7:18f.; 8:28f.) and his desire simply to glorify (12:28; 17:4) and please God (8:29).[13]

---

[12] Carson, 95.
[13] Walter A. Elwell, editor, *Evangelical Commentary on the Bible* (Grand Rapids: Baker Book House, 1989), 869.

This unique relationship is also illustrated in the important sub-theme of the Father sending the Son on His mission.[14] John establishes the mission of the Son in his prologue: the eternal Logos is in the bosom of the Father and is sent forth to reveal God in flesh.[15] Hebrew religion understood this sender/messenger relationship in the *shaliach* principle: "One sent is as he who sends him." The "messenger is viewed as the representative of the sender," thus having the authority and dignity of the one who sent him. Through obedience to the sender, the credibility and legitimacy of the messenger is established.[16]

Both the submission of purpose and the full authority of the one sent are found in the mission of Christ. John said it this way:

> Then Jesus, still teaching in the temple courts, cried out, "Yes, you know me, and you know where I am from. I am not here on my own, but he who sent me is true. You do not know him, but I know him because I am from him and he sent me"—John 7:28-29

> For I have come down from heaven not to do my will but to do the will of him who sent me. And this is the will of him who sent me, that I shall lose none of all that he has given me, but raise them up at the last day. For my Father's will is that everyone who looks to the Son and believes in him shall have eternal life, and I will raise him up at the last day.—John 6:38-40

As deity, the Son knows the Father intimately. In His humanity, the Son is submitted to the will of the Father. No closer relationship can be achieved than one of perfect understanding and agreement of will.

Although Christ was in total submission to the Father as the one who sent Him, we must be careful not to confuse submission of purpose in His humanity with subordination of nature in His deity. Christ is God in the fullest sense of deity. God has only one will. (To say that there are separate wills among the Persons of the Trinity, is to say there are three Gods [tritheism]).

---

[14] Beasley-Murray wrote in *Gospel of Life: Theology in the Fourth Gospel* (Peabody: Hendrickson Publishers, 1991), 15-16: "Bultmann counted seventeen examples of the participial phrase 'he who sent me' (ho pempsas me), plus six occurrences of the expression 'the Father who sent me' (with the same verb); and he noted fifteen corresponding statements in which the synonymous verb apostellein, 'send out,' is used. From R. Bultmann, *Gospel of John*, trans. G. R. Beasley-Murray et al. (Oxford: Blackwell, 1971) 249, n.2.

[15] John 1:1-18, primarily vs. 14 and 18. So Wisdom in Proverbs 8 is "in the beginning," was "brought forth," "whoever finds me finds life" and yet is always with the Father.

[16] Note, for instance, how David's messenges represented David in 2 Samuel 10. Their humiliation was David's humiliation.

Summary

This theme supports the deity of Christ. Jesus Christ is the "one and only" Son at the Father's side who has come to reveal God to us. All that Christ did was to glorify the Father.

Access to the Father is direct since Christ has united us together with Him and the Father. In John 16:26-28, Jesus declared, "In that day you will ask in my name. I am not saying that I will ask the Father on your behalf. No, the Father himself loves you because you have loved me and have believed that I came from God. I came from the Father and entered the world; now I am leaving the world and going back to the Father."

The unity of the Father and Son is to be the model for our unity (Jn. 17:21). The love that the Father had for His Son is the kind of love He gives to us:

> How great is the love the Father has lavished on us, that we should be called children of God! And that is what we are! The reason the world does not know us is that it did not know him.—1 John 3:1

The love and obedience of the Son to the Father is a model for our paternal relationships.

Application

Do you have a hard time coming to the Father in prayer? Do you have trouble imagining His love reaching out to you from the throne? Is your love for Jesus more than your love for the Father? Can you pray to Christ, but not to the Father? Explain.

If you answered "yes" to any of the above, then perhaps your image of the Father is wrong. Consider the following.

What we see reflected in the life of Christ is the heart of the Father. The love, compassion, and caring we so readily relate to in Christ is also the same love, compassion, and caring that comes from the Father. There is no difference. When we look at Christ, we are looking at the Father. "To know Him is to know the Father" (Jn. 8:19). Some people cannot relate to the Father except as some overbearing tyrant who demands perfection before He throws us a morsel of love.

We should not think of the Father as an abusive tyrant, or even unforgiving. The Father is long-suffering, sending numerous warnings for the people to repent. God is slow to wrath. His purpose in judgment is always for deliverance.

Comment on the following:
1. Christ was confident of the Father's approval (Jn. 3:35; 8:16).

2. Christ had great zeal for the Father (Jn. 2:16-17).

3. Christ was energized by the Father (Jn. 4:34; 6:57).

4. Christ was a Father-pleaser, not a crowd-pleaser (Jn. 7:16-19).

5. Christ was a Father-revealer (Jn. 17:20-26).

Application (Continued)

Do you harbor any bitterness, self-pity, or resentment as a result of your relationship to your father? How does the Father/Son relationship in the Gospel of John challenge those feelings? Have you forgiven your father?

Further principles applied to parents:

1. *As the Father worked, so the Son worked.* Our children learn what we value and often follow us in career choices. They usually have abilities that match our own. What kind of work ethic have you taught your children?

2. *The Son speaks the things He sees the Father doing.* Our children esteem our actions and often talk about them. Explain the phrase, "But daddy does it!"

3. *The words that the Father gives, the Son gives to others.* Our children learn our vocabularies and habits of speech. What have our children learned to tell the world?

4. *All that belonged to the Father, also belonged to the Son.* Fathers must be ready to share or give to their children as needed and right. Do you resent giving your children time, money, or possessions? Explain.

5. *To not honor the Son is to not honor the Father.* Children bear your name and your honor. If you neglect your children, you are neglecting your honor. Explain your relationship with your children. Do your children know that you approve of them? (See John 6:27.)

Application (Continued)

6. *If you have seen the Son, you have seen the Father.* Your children reflect you in looks, actions, manners, and behavior. They are a reflection of your strengths and weaknesses. If you want to know the way children really are, look at their parents. (And vice-a-versa.) Explain some ways in which your children reflect you.

7. *Because of the intimate relationship of the Father and the Son, the Son was able to stand alone.* Having an intimate, singular character example is a necessary prerequisite to standing alone. The ability to stand alone comes by knowing that we are not alone (the Lord is always with us). The motivation to stand alone must be based on loving the Lord. Fathers must be protectors, providers, and sharers with their children. Only when children stand alone can parents expand their freedom with confidence that they will not abuse it (Song 8:8-9). Are your children able to stand alone?

3

The Trial Theme

Bible Review

Read through the following verses. Pay careful attention to the terms and ideas of a trial.

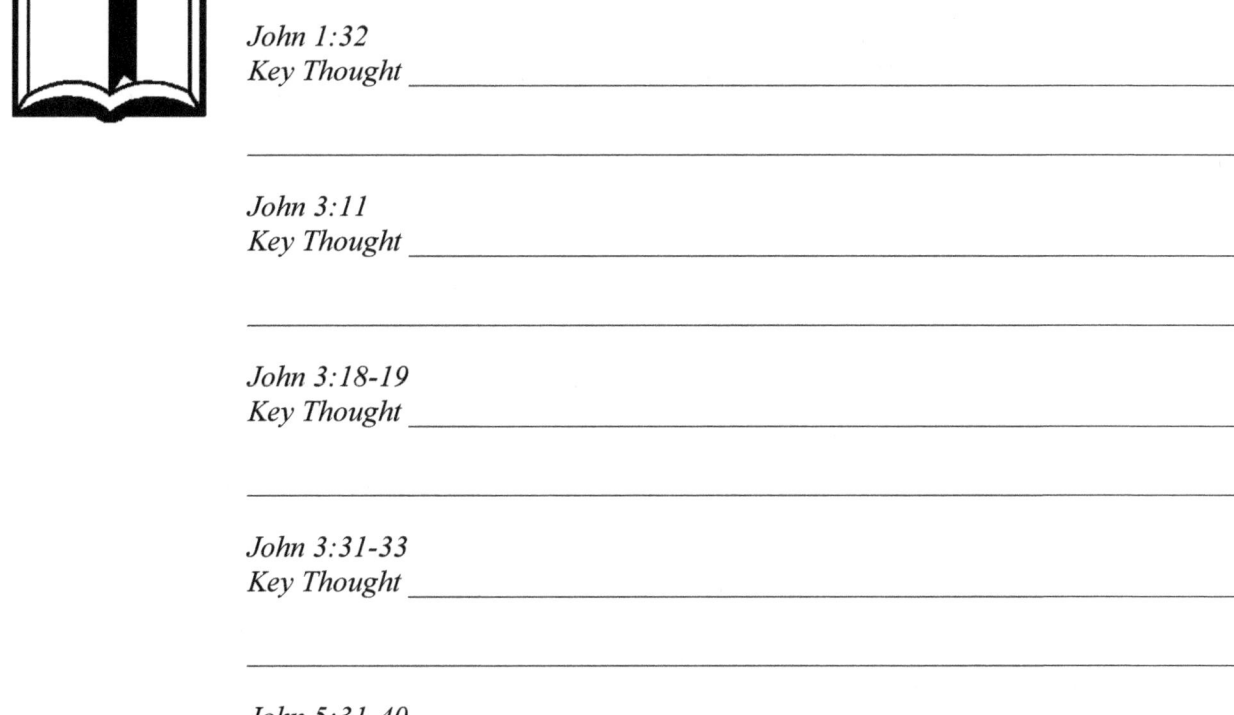

Key Scriptures

John 1:32
Key Thought _____
_____

John 3:11
Key Thought _____
_____

John 3:18-19
Key Thought _____
_____

John 3:31-33
Key Thought _____
_____

John 5:31-40
Key Thought _____
_____

John 5:45
Key Thought _____
_____

Key Scriptures

Jn. 8:12-18
Key Thought _____

_____

_____

John 8:50
Key Thought _____

_____

John 9:16-24 (See Joshua 7:19.)
Key Thought _____

_____

_____

Jn. 15:22-24
Key Thought _____

_____

John 16:7b-11
Key Thought _____

_____

_____

Jn. 19:33-35
Key Thought _____

_____

_____

Jn. 21:24
Key Thought _____

_____

Comments and Analysis

1. What terms does John use that remind you of a trial?

2. How does the Apostle John verify that Christ is who He said He was? Who bears witness of Christ? What is certified (sealed)?

3. Does this support the apologetic purpose of John's Gospel? Does this help verify the deity of Christ? Explain.

4. List below the four evidences that Jesus gives in John 5:33-40 that He is who He says He is:
   1. _____
   2. _____
   3. _____
   4. _____

5. How do Isaiah 41:21-23, 27; 43:26, 44:8 and Jeremiah 23:16-18 relate to John's trial theme?

Review of John's Trial Theme

Throughout his gospel, the apostle John weaves the theme of *humankind on trial*. "The motif of a trial runs through the entire gospel like a scarlet thread."[17] In effect, John tells the story of Jesus in terms of a cosmic lawsuit. Andrew Lincoln agrees, "But perhaps, second only to the narrative's unique Christology, this metaphor of a lawsuit on a cosmic scale is the most distinctive characteristic holding many of the elements of its plot and discourse together."[18]

On the surface we see the actual events of Christ on trial, but just underneath John places humankind before the Judge. Christ has presented His case (Jn. 15:22). The evidence is clear. Christ is the Son of God, the Savior of the world. Humankind has been arraigned and sentenced. The Judge has given Christ the power to carry out the sentencing (Jn. 5:22). But Christ has made a plea for us. Will humankind accept the commuted sentence? We all have the choice to be saved from judgment by receiving Christ, or to be condemned by rejecting Him.

> Whoever believes in him is not condemned, but whoever does not believe stands condemned already because he has not believed in the name of God's one and only Son. —Jn. 3:18

> The one who comes from heaven is above all. He testifies to what he has seen and heard, but no one accepts his testimony...The Father loves the Son and has placed everything in his hands. Whoever believes in the Son has eternal life, but whoever rejects the Son will not see life, for God's wrath remains on him.—Jn. 3:31b-32, 35-36

When we view the gospel from this trial theme, we see that the Prologue acts as a trial summary statement—or attorney's opening argument—that John will prove in the rest of his gospel. The accused are all the unbelievers that, like the reader, weigh the evidence, hear the verdict and decide whether they will receive the commuted sentence or not. Their decision determines whether they will receive mercy or judgment.

The Book of Signs (Jn. 1:19-12:50), which includes many of Christ's miracles, becomes the "courtroom" evidence proving Christ's claims. At the end of this section (Jn. 12:37-50), the "defense rests" as John gives a closing argument to summarize the results of the evidence.

Throughout the gospel, John gives us the judge, the advocates, the witnesses, the charges, the evidence, the interrogations, the verdict, and the sentencing of the "Trial of the Ages."

The Judge and the Advocates

The Father is portrayed as the Judge (Jn. 8:50, 54; 12:47-48) and Jesus Christ as the Judge Advocate (Jn. 5:28-30, 45-46; cf. 1 Jn. 2:1). Christ initiates the lawsuit with humankind as God's representative (Jn. 5:36), but judging is a joint enterprise for the Father and Son (Jn. 8:16, 18). In fact, the Father set His seal on Christ (Jn. 3:33)—as one who seals a legal document—thus showing the approval of Christ as the representative of the court of heaven.

---

[17] Blank, *Krisis*, p. 310. Cited in Beasley-Murray, 61.
[18] Andrew T. Lincoln, *Truth on Trial: the Lawsuit Motif in the Fourth Gospel* (Peabody: Hendrickson Publishers, 2000) 13.

Into this trial of the ages enters the Holy Spirit—the Counselor or Advocate who convicts the world. The Holy Spirit is the advocate for the prosecution (Jn. 15:18-16:11).[19] The Greek word for Counselor is "parakletos." The word means "one called alongside" and speaks of the counseling, teaching, and helping aspects of the Holy Spirit. However, "Parakletos primarily means 'legal assistant, advocate,' someone who helps another in court, whether as an advocate, a witness, or a representative...the Paraklete serves rather more as a prosecuting attorney than as counsel for the defense. 'Counselor' is not wrong, so long as 'legal counselor' is understood, not camp counselor' or 'marriage counselor.'"[20] "Advocate" is essentially a forensic term.

What is the world guilty of? It is guilty of its sin, its (hypocritical) righteousness, and its (unjust) judgment. The Holy Spirit points His divine finger at the hearts of the unrighteous and says, "You are guilty." Gary Burge notes, "He substantiates our witness (another legal term) as we too are placed on trial before the world."[21] Even the Greek word for "convict" (elencho) is "legal terminology for the trial."[22]

The Witnesses and Evidence

"A witness[23] is a person who tells others what he knows of a certain event that has occurred. He seeks to establish facts by the information he has acquired from personal experience. The object of the witness is to persuade others that certain statements are true or false." However, it is necessary to have more than one witness to convict someone. Gary Burge comments, "In Jewish law one witness (even a man witnessing of himself [vv.30-31]) was insufficient either to condemn or confirm a charge (Deut. 17:6; Mish Kethuboth 2:9)."[24] Two or more were necessary.

Witness is an important term in the Fourth Gospel. "The noun witness or testimony occurs fourteen times in this Gospel in comparison with four times in the three Synoptics together, and the verb to witness or to testify thirty-three times in comparison with twice in the three Synoptics."[25]

John marshals several witnesses before us in his gospel. Each one testifies about Christ. There was the voice of the Father. There was the appearance of the Holy Spirit descending like a dove on Christ at His baptism (Jn. 1:32).[26] There was also the testimony of John the Baptist, who saw the Holy Spirit as a dove descend on Christ.

There was even the blind man who had been given sight by Christ. He scolded the religious leaders for not seeing Christ for who He is. "Now that is remarkable! You don't know where he comes from, yet he opened my eyes" (Jn. 9:30).

The Old Testament Scriptures bear witness of Christ. Numerous prophecies have been fulfilled in Christ. Even the disbelief of the Jews was prophesied:

---

[19] This role is not to be confused with the "accuser of the brothers" (Rev. 12:10).
[20] Carson, 499.
[21] Walter A. Elwell, editor, *Evangelical Commentary on the Bible* (Grand Rapids: Baker Book House, 1989) 871.
[22] Op. cit., 871.
[23] John uses the noun for "witness" 14 times and the verb 33 times—more than any other New Testament writer does.
[24] Op. cit., 854.
[25] Lincoln, 12.
[26] John declared in his first epistle, "The Spirit is the witness because the Spirit is the truth" (1 Jn. 5:6).

> Even after Jesus had done all these miraculous signs in their presence, they still would not believe in him. This was to fulfill the word of Isaiah the prophet: "Lord, who has believed our message and to whom has the arm of the Lord been revealed?"—John 12:37-38

The miracles of Christ proved His power over nature and death. From the first miracle of changing the water to wine in Cana to the resurrection of Lazarus, Christ proved His authority and power.

There was the testimony of Christ's disciples—whose writings and changed lives continue to bear witness. Let us not forget John himself, who declared, "These are written that you may believe that Jesus is the Christ and that by believing you may have life in His name" (Jn. 20:31; cf. Jn. 21:24).

As we noted earlier, John summarized these witnesses in Chapter 5:31-40. John expounds on these witnesses in several other passages as well:

- The witness of the Father - Jn. 12:28.

- The witness of John the Baptist - Jn. 1:15-19. Burge notes, "The Fourth Gospel takes great pains to affirm that the Baptist was *not* the Messiah (John 1:20; 3:28), that he was not the light (1:8f.), and that Jesus is superior (1:30; 3:29f.; 10:41). We even witness disciples of John the Baptist becoming Jesus' first converts (1:35-42)."[27]

- The witness of His works - Jn. 2:9; 3:14; 4:29, 51; 6:2, 11, 19; 9:6-7; 11:43-44; 20:9; 21:6.

- The witness of the Scriptures - Jn. 1:11; 12:15; 15:25; 19:24, 28, 34, 36, 41; 20:9.

There was also the witness of Christ Himself. His mission consisted not only of judging but also of bearing witness to the truth (Jn. 5:20-39; 8:13-18; 18:37). His words and actions were a consistent support—evidence—for the veracity of His testimony:

Words	**Actions**
Claimed to have the words of the Father (Jn. 8:28).	Spoke supernatural truth to the Samaritan woman at the well (Jn. 4).
Claimed to be the Bread of Life.	Fed the multitudes (Jn. 6).
Claimed to be the Light of the World.	Healed the blind man (Jn. 9).
Claimed to be the Good Shepherd.	Laid down His life for the sheep (Jn. 10).
Claimed to be the Resurrection and the Life.	Raised Lazarus from the dead (Jn. 11).

---

[27] Elwell, 845. Note how the trial language plays out in the interrogations/testimonies given by John: Interrogation (Jn. 1:19-28) then Testimony (Jn. 1:29-35); Interrogation (Jn. 3:22-36) then Testimony (of what it means to "receive" (Jn. 3:32-33, 36).

Since Christ always spoke the truth that was given Him from the Father, He could bear witness of Himself.

> When Jesus spoke again to the people, he said, "I am the light of the world. Whoever follows me will never walk in darkness, but will have the light of life." The Pharisees challenged him, "Here you are, appearing as your own witness; your testimony is not valid." Jesus answered, "Even if I testify on my own behalf, my testimony is valid, for I know where I came from and where I am going. But you have no idea where I come from or where I am going. You judge by human standards; I pass judgment on no one. But if I do judge, my decisions are right, because I am not alone. I stand with the Father, who sent me. In your own Law it is written that the testimony of two men is valid. I am one who testifies for myself; my other witness is the Father, who sent me."
> —John 8:12-18

We should also note that Christ often introduced His testimony with the words, "Amen, Amen" (or "Verily, Verily;" Jn. 3:11; 5:24, etc.). The "double Amen formula...occurs twenty-five times as an introduction to his words, serves as a swearing ritual in this juridical context, and is unique to this Gospel."[28]

Christ's own resurrection was the final vindication of all He said about Himself. (For more information regarding Christ as witness, see Appendix D, *Christ as the Faithful and True Witness*.)

There is a large contingent of other individuals who confirm that Jesus is the Son of God. These include the disciples, Samaritans, and multitudes: Jn. 1:40-41, 45, 49; 4:41-42; 6:14, 68-69; 7:31, 40-41; 9:35-38; 10:33; 11:27, 45; 12:11, 42; 19:7; 20:8, 20, 27-28.

Finally, the gospel itself stands as a court document, or witness, for or against the world. John 21:24 states, "This is the disciple who *testifies to these things and who wrote them down*. We know that his testimony is true" (emphasis added).

The Charges and Interrogations

Not only does the Fourth Gospel provide this overwhelming testimony declaring the identity of Christ, but Christ, as God in human flesh, testified that the world was evil. Jesus said, "The world cannot hate you, but it hates me because *I testify that what it does is evil*." (John 7:7). Such statements form part of the charges, or accusations, of Christ against the world (Jn. 5:37-47; 8:12-59; cf. Is. 11:2-5).[29]

At one point, Jesus also enlists the witness of Moses who will become Israel's accuser in the future age:

> "But do not think I will accuse you before the Father. Your accuser is Moses,[30] on whom your hopes are set. If you believed Moses, you would believe me, for he wrote about me. But since you do not believe what he wrote, how are you going to believe what I say?"
> —Jn. 5:45-47

---

[28] Lincoln, 30.
[29] See Appendix D, Christ as the Faithful and True Witness. Note that the Greek work for "persecute" (διώκω) can be translated "put on trial" in forensic contexts.
[30] ὁ κατηγορῶν ὑμῶν Μωϋσῆς

The religious rulers also leveled charges against Christ, accusing him, for example, of being a false prophet (Jn. 7:47-52). "The Jews' have three other main charges against Jesus, arising from their understanding of the law. He is a violator of the Sabbath laws and therefore a sinner (cf. 5:16; 7:23; 9:16, 24). He is a blasphemer, attempting to make himself equal to God (cf. 5:17, 18; 10:30-39; cf. also 8:58, 59). And finally, he is an enemy of the Jewish nation"[31] (Jn. 11:46-53).

In this sense they fulfill the role of court interrogators—on a worldly level. But all such accusations and judgments of humankind pale in light of the court of heaven. Here is the greatest irony: in their zeal for the law, they were blind to the presence of the Lawgiver who stood before them, accusing them.

Several discourses in John actually become court interrogations (Jn. 8-9). The interrogation of the man born blind (Jn. 9) follows this form. In this discourse the religious rulers ask the man born blind how he came to see, then they ask his parents, then they ask him again, not willing to acknowledge a miracle. In fact, they state, "Give glory to God! We know this man is a sinner" (Jn. 9:24). It seems that the verdict of guilty was already in their minds. And by giving the admonition to "Give glory to God!" they were declaring a "call to confess or admit the truth, putting the witness under solemn oath"[32] (cf. Josh. 7:19), thus preparing the man for their final judgment. They ask the blind man a third time how he was healed, hurl insults at him for his refusal to back down, and then excommunicate him.

The discourse of Christ and the religious rulers in John 8 also follows the form of an interrogation. We will pause here only to note one important thing. Jesus uses the words "I am" (*ego eimi*) without a predicate (cf. 8:24, 28, 58; 18:5, 8). This follows Isaiah 43:10, where Yahweh makes the same claim about Himself in his lawsuit with Israel.[33]

Christ clearly understood His role as the Divine Judge Advocate of the court of heaven and answered His interrogators just as God did to Israel in the ancient lawsuit.

The Verdict and Sentencing

Somewhere in the eternal heavenlies, God struck His great gavel of justice for all humankind. The overwhelming testimony and evidence proves beyond any doubt that Christ is the Son of God. His unique Light exposed the depravity of all humankind, who now have no excuse (Jn. 15:22-25). The verdict has been decided: those who reject Christ remain condemned (Jn. 3:18). The sentence is the same for all: God's eternal wrath (Jn. 3:36).

But just as the gavel struck, the Son stood beside the convicted and declared, "I will take the punishment." What the world saw as unrighteousness—the lifting up of Christ on the cross—was, in fact, the righteousness of God. Christ has forever paid the penalty for our sins. For those who believe (those who accept Christ's witness), the Father has reversed the verdict and commuted the sentence.

---

[31] Op. Cit., 24. The rulers also interrogated John the Baptist (Jn. 1:19-28).
[32] Op. Cit., 100.
[33] Andrew Lincoln (p. 40) states, "In this connection, the LXX version of Deutero-Isaiah frequently employs the ego eimi, 'I am,' formula for Yahweh's self-predication as the one true God. It occurs four times in the trial speeches (cf. 41:4; 43:10, 25; 45:18), with 43:10 being particularly striking because of its reference to the people of Israel as witnesses who understand that 'I am.' But the formula in this absolute form is also found in 46:4 (twice), 48:12, and 51:12."

Condemnation is imminent. The danger of eternal judgment is definite and real.[34] Will we be like the religious leaders who sought to extinguish that Light, or will we be like Thomas who fell at His feet and received the commuted sentence when he declared, "My Lord, and my God" (Jn. 20:28)?

The Holy Spirit and Our Task as Witnesses

As we noted earlier, the Holy Spirit prosecutes the case for Christ against the world. In other words, as we speak the gospel testimony, the Holy Spirit guides us and, in fact, personally testifies through us (1 Jn. 5:6; cf. Mt. 10:16-20). A. A. Trites commented on the earthly advocacy role:

> While he was on earth, Jesus bore witness to the truth and served as the chief advocate for God in the world (18:37; 10:34-38; 14:10-11; 18:23). Now his juridical functions are taken over by "another Paraclete," the Holy Spirit promised by Jesus (14:16–18).[35]

First of all, the Holy Spirit exposes and convicts the world of sin, because the world refuses to believe in Christ; secondly of righteousness, because Christ's ascension vindicated His testimony as righteous; and lastly of judgment, because those who reject Christ and follow Satan are condemned with him.

Just as it would be necessary for the evidence in a trial to be truthful to bring any authentic, convicting effect, so the advocacy ministry of the Holy Spirit must be grounded in the truth. To this end, Christ described the Spirit as "the Spirit of Truth" (Jn. 14:17; 15:26; 16:13) who "will guide you into all truth" (Jn. 16:13). Similarly, for our witness to carry any weight in the courts of men's hearts, we must bear testimony based on the Spirit's revealed truth—both objective truth, based on Scripture, and subjective truth, based on the present revelation of the Holy Spirit.

In this role, then, the Holy Spirit acts as a joint *witness* with us (Jn. 15:26-27; Acts 1:8; 1 Jn. 5:6-9), testifying on behalf of Christ and enabling us to testify aligned with Christ's truth. Andrew Lincoln notes, "Just as Jesus has been the Father's authorized agent as witness in the trial, so now the disciples are to be Jesus' authorized agents as they bear witness in the trial of truth that is still taking place"[36] (Jn. 17:18). This authorization to be witnesses comes with the backing of the Holy Spirit who continues to convict the world of sin, righteousness, and judgment through us.

---

[34] The sealed judgment scroll is handed to Christ by the Judge in Revelation 5.
[35] A. A. Trites, *Witness*, in Joel G.Green, Scot McKnight, I. Howard Marshall, editors, *Dictionary of Jesus and the Gospels* (Downer's Grove, IL: InterVarsity Press, 1998) 879.
[36] Lincoln, 27.

Application

1. Comment on the following: The trial has to do with determining who is right.

2. Explain how Christians are on trial and how the world is on trial.

3. How is the world guilty of its righteousness and judgment?

4. What does the Holy Spirit convict the world of? How is this illustrated in Acts 2:37?

5. How does the Holy Spirit convict the world? If the Holy Spirit is our Advocate before unbelievers, how does this affect our ability in evangelism? Should we use the witnesses of John's Gospel in evangelism?

6. Have you seen the evidence of the Holy Spirit convict someone? Do we sometimes try to do the work of the Holy Spirit? Explain.

7. Comment on the following: "Where the world rejects the testimony, their 'joy' at being rid of Jesus (John 16:20) is, in Blank's words, 'the joy of the damned.'[37] Where the testimony is received they experience the joy of the forgiven."[38]

---

[37] Blank, *Krisis*, 338. Cited in Beasley-Murray, 77.

4

The Conflict Theme (Belief and Unbelief)

Bible Review

Read through the following verses. Pay careful attention to the conflict between belief and unbelief, between light and darkness.

Key Scriptures

John 1:4-7
Key Thought _____

_____

John 1:11
Key Thought _____

_____

John 3:18-21
Key Thought _____

_____

Jn. 8:12
Key Thought _____

_____

John 12:35-36a
Key Thought _____

_____

John 12:37
Key Thought _____

_____

John 12:44-46
Key Thought _____

_____

---
[38] Beasley-Murray, 77.

Comments and Analysis

1. Describe the conflict illustrated in these verses.

2. Are light and truth, and darkness and unbelief synonyms?

3. Why do people choose darkness? Who rejected Christ? What problems will you have if you walk in darkness? Why do some people want the light?

4. What does light expose? Why can't darkness understand light? Why does darkness oppose light?

5. What are the consequences of belief and unbelief? Comment on Ephesians 5:8-14.

6. What or who is truth? What must you believe to stay in the light?

7. How do these verses support John's overall theme?

Review of John's Conflict Theme

John uses the conflict between faith and unbelief to reveal the Person of Christ and bring the reader into eternal life.[39] "All the signs, teachings, and events in the Gospel are used to stimulate faith in Christ and are so ordered that they mark growth in this faith on the part of his disciples."[40] The reader follows the conflict and watches the growth of faith in the disciples and the growth of unbelief in those who reject Christ. Likewise, as the miracles of Jesus grow in intensity, so the hatred and denial grows in the hearts of those who oppose Him.[41] "The conflict between belief and unbelief, exemplified in the actions and utterances of the main characters, forms the plot."[42] This progression ultimately leads to two things central to this plot:

- The false triumph of the religious leaders who crucified Christ.

- The vindication of belief in Christ through the resurrection.

This theme is also depicted as the conflict between the symbols of light and darkness. Christ is the Light and brings light (truth) through His actions and words. He declared, "I am the light of the world. Whoever follows me will never walk in darkness, but will have the light of life" (Jn. 8:12). Just as darkness cannot understand light and cannot overcome it, so the religious and political systems of Christ's day cannot overcome Him. The "light keeps on giving light" and darkness cannot "lay hold of" or "master" it (Greek, katalambano).[43] When light shines, the darkness flees!

Belief and Unbelief Illustrated in Several Events

Unbelief was expressed toward Christ primarily at His home, where a prophet is without honor (Jn. 1:11; 4:44; cf. Lk. 13:31-35) and at Jerusalem, a place which has consistently rejected the godly people sent there (Acts 7:51-52). (See Appendix A, *Locating the Belief/Unbelief Conflict*, for further details.) Gary Burge noted, "The transition from Jerusalem to Galilee is a transition from unbelief to belief, from darkness to light."[44]

Each of the major discourses in the Fourth Gospel describes "a different personality with a different need and a different challenge to faith."[45] Nicodemus had to reconcile his religious status and thinking to being born again into the kingdom of God (Jn. 3:1-15). The woman at the well in Samaria had to reconcile her prejudice and sexual sin to the authority of the Messiah (Jn. 4:1-26). The paralytic had to choose to follow tradition or obedience to Jesus for healing (Jn. 5:1-15). The former blind man faced the wrath of the synagogue if he chose to support his Healer (Jn. 9:1-38). Each one had to overcome these challenges for faith to be released in their lives.

---

[39] The word "faith" occurs ninety-eight times in John's Gospel. It is more frequent than any other important subject is.
[40] F. E. Gaebelein, editor, *The Expositor's Bible Commentary*, vol. 9, (Grand Rapids: Zondervan Publishing House, 1981) 12.
[41] Tenney notes on page 17 of the *Expositor's Bible Commentary*, vol. 9, that there are at least "six conflicts with 'the Jews' (2:18-20; 5:16-47; 6:41-59; 7:15-44; 8:31-58; 10:22-39)." To this we should add the seventh and final conflict at Christ's passion.
[42] Op. cit., 12.
[43] A. T. Robertson, *Word Pictures in the New Testament*, vol. 5, (Nashville: Broadman Press, 1932) 7.
[44] Burge, 853.
[45] Tenney, 13.

Even the disciples had to choose to believe in Christ when the rest of the crowds turned away (Jn. 6:1-69). Their faith faltered during the hour of darkness, but Christ warned them—preparing them in advance—and prayed for them to be steadfast (Jn. 16:32-33; Jn. 17:9-11). His promises and prayers became a source of faith (Jn. 14:28-29).

Faith Gained From Miracles

Faith was gained by those who believed in Jesus through the demonstration of His supernatural power. John records seven miracles performed by Christ (other than Christ's own resurrection):

1. Turned Water to Wine – John 2:9
2. Healed the Nobleman's Son – Jn. 4:51
3. Healed the Invalid – Jn. 5:8-9
4. Fed the 5,000 – Jn. 6:10-11
5. Walked on Water – Jn. 6:19
6. Healed the Blind Man – Jn. 9:6-7
7. Raised Lazarus From the Dead – Jn. 11:43-44

The miracles of Christ lead us step-by-step to a conclusion that Christ is the Son of God. He had power over the physical body, power over nature, and ultimately, power over life and death.

John records ample signs sufficient for belief. Yet Christ was challenged by conflict with unbelief everywhere He turned. The power of Christ's miracles actually revealed the true motivation behind the religious rulers: fear of losing power. When Christ made an appeal for the Jews to believe in Him based on the evidence of His miracles, the Jews sought to arrest Him:

> Do not believe me unless I do what my Father does. But if I do it, even though you do not believe me, believe the miracles, that you may know and understand that the Father is in me, and I in the Father." Again they tried to seize him, but he escaped their grasp.
> —John 10:37-39

John remarked about the Jew's unbelief:

> Even after Jesus had done all these miraculous signs in their presence, they still would not believe in him…For this reason they could not believe, because, as Isaiah says elsewhere: "He has blinded their eyes and deadened their hearts, so they can neither see with their eyes, nor understand with their hearts, nor turn—and I would heal them"…Yet at the same time many even among the leaders believed in him. But because of the Pharisees they would not confess their faith for fear they would be put out of the synagogue; for they loved praise from men more than praise from God.—John 12:37, 39-40, 42-43

This prompted from Christ a bold, but final appeal to the Jews for faith:

> Then Jesus cried out, "When a man believes in me, he does not believe in me only, but in the one who sent me. When he looks at me, he sees the one who sent me. I have come into the world as a light, so that no one who believes in me should stay in darkness."
> —Jn. 12:44-46

With the crucifixion of Christ, unbelief seemed to envelop belief. But even when darkness seemed to triumph, the light of Christ was vindicated. Christ rose from the dead.

Summary

The following general outline summarizes the progress of belief and unbelief in John's Gospel:

Scripture	Summary
Jn. 1:1-18	Prologue - Faith set forth
Jn. 1:19-12:50	Miracle narratives and discourses - Growth and conflict of faith and unbelief
Jn. 13:1-17:26	Personal discipleship - Faith strengthened
Jn. 18:1-19, 42	Crucifixion - Hour of unbelief
Jn. 20:1-31	Resurrection appearances - Vindication and triumph of faith
Jn. 21:1-25	Epilogue - Faith continues

(See Appendix B, *Belief/Unbelief Conflict in John's Gospel*, for a more complete outline of the conflict between belief and unbelief.)

Merrill C. Tenney commented,

> Perhaps the greatest theological contribution of the Gospel is a full discussion and demonstration of the nature of belief. Both by definition and by example its essence is described. Belief is equated with receiving (1:12), following (1:40), drinking (fig., 4:13), responding (4:51), eating (fig., 6:57), accepting (6:60, lit. "hear"), worship (9:38), obeying (11:39-41), and commitment (12:10-11). The lives of those who "believed" show both the method and result of their faith.[46]

Whether confronting individuals or crowds, whether clashing with tradition or the Jewish hierarchy, Christ, the Light of Life, illumined hearts and challenged darkness on every hand. Christ's triumph left faith in the Son of God secure and the light of life available to all.

---

[46] Gaebelein, 18.

Application

1. What do Jesus' personal interviews reveal to us about Himself? Did Jesus reach out to various classes in society? Does this broaden the apologetic appeal of John's Gospel?

2. Is faith merely rational persuasion (Jn. 6:44)? Explain. How do the miracles of Christ affect your faith?

3. Comment on the following: Following the Light is the harder decision to make.

4. Comment on the following: The more light you give, the more conflict you receive.

5. What challenges to faith have you had to overcome?

6. Comment on the following: Light is stronger than darkness.

Application

7. Why are night clubs almost always dimly lit? Is unbelief sin? Explain.

8. Is the light available to everyone (Jn. 1:9)? Why do some remain in darkness? Comment on the following: "One is either attracted to or repulsed by the light."[47]

9. How was the Apostle John a "light-revealer?" What can we do to bring the light of life to others?

10. Comment on the following: "Only a real risk tests the reality of a belief."[48]

---

[47] Elwell, 851.
[48] Wayne Martindale and Jerry Root, editors, *The Quotable Lewis* (Wheaton: Tyndale House Publishers, 1989) 67.

5

Old Testament Themes in John's Prologue

Bible Review

Review John's prologue (Jn. 1:1-18). Note the following terms as you read: Word, beginning, light, darkness, life, dwelling/tabernacle, glory, grace, law, and one and only (or some translations – begotten). Then read these Old Testament Scriptures and note any similarities.

Key Scriptures

Ps. 104:24
Key Thought _____

_____

Prov. 8:1, 35-36
Key Thought _____

_____

Is. 55:11
Key Thought _____

_____

Ge. 1:1-4
Key Thought _____

_____

Ps. 33:6
Key Thought _____

_____

Ex. 40:34-35
Key Thought _____

_____

Ex. 33:18-22; 34:5-6
Key Thought _____

_____

_____

Comments and Analysis

1. List below several words in these Old Testament passages that are reminiscent of John's prologue. List next to them the corresponding New Testament words.

2. What words are personified in the Old Testament? What words are personified in the New Testament?

3. When God revealed His glory, what was declared about His nature?

4. What must Christ do to reveal the glory of God? Is there any essential difference between the glory of the Father and the glory of the Son? Explain.

5. Comment on the relationship between the Old and New Testaments.

6. What does John say is different between what Moses provided and what Jesus provides?

7. What is grace?

Review of John's Use of the Old Testament in the Prologue

John's prologue is not just the summary statement for the themes in the Fourth Gospel. It is also the gathering point of many important themes from the Old Testament. Several streams of revelation in the Old Testament unite in these eighteen verses of beautiful rhythmical prose. These revelations become the background of Christ's pre-incarnate nature, including the relationship between the Father and Son, and are the foundation of God's purpose to "in-flesh" the Word, reveal the Light, and overcome darkness.

Christ's Pre-incarnate Nature

John uses the Greek term *logos* to describe the nature and mission of Christ. We translate this term as "word," but it has to do both with the thoughts of God and the creative force of those thoughts as they are spoken forth. John Calvin explained, "Just as men's speech is called the expression of their thought, so it is not inappropriate to say that God expressed himself to us by his speech or 'Word.'"[49] Perhaps "word in action"[50] best summarizes the meaning of logos.

Logos is personified and signifies that when God created the worlds, it was through Christ.[51] In the Old Testament this is put in several different terms. In Genesis, God speaks the creation into existence: "in the beginning...God said." The Psalmist agrees, "By the word of the Lord are the heavens made" (Ps. 33:6). In Proverbs 8, wisdom "calls out" and is the "craftsman" by the side of God during creation. Finding this wisdom results in finding life.

It is not surprising, then, that we find John describing the pre-incarnate Christ as this same personified agency of creation: "Through him all things were made; without him nothing was made that has been made" (John 1:3). D. A. Carson writes:

> In short, God's "Word" in the Old Testament is his powerful self-expression in creation, revelation and salvation, and the personification of that "Word" makes it suitable for John to apply it as a title to God's ultimate self-disclosure, the person of his own Son.[52]

Incarnated Light Overcomes Darkness

Just as wisdom brings life (Prov. 8), so "In him was life, and that life was the light of men" (John 1:4). Just as light is not static, but always moving, so the Light of God has taken on flesh and continues to reveal God to mankind. Just as light casts out darkness, so "The light shines in the darkness, but the darkness has not understood it" (Jn. 1:5). Just as it was necessary for God to speak into the darkness in creation, "Let there be light" (Ge. 1:3), so it is necessary for His Word to speak into our hearts to bring the light of truth. The God who is revealed in Christ "illuminates those who believe and drives back the darkness of evil. The repulsion of darkness is the *judgment* of the world."[53] John shows us the defeat of darkness in his gospel.

---

[49] A. McGrath and J. I. Packer, editors, *John* (Wheaton: Crossway Books, 1994) 13.
[50] F. F. Bruce, *The Gospel of John* (Grand Rapids: Eerdmans, 1983) 29.
[51] See Col. 1:15-18, which is a word study on "Berishith" (in the beginning) the first word of the Hebrew Bible, and Rev. 3:14, where Christ is the "origin" of the creation of God. See also, C. F. Burney, *Christ as the APXH of Creation*, **The Journal of Theological Studies**, 27, 1926, pp. 160-177.
[52] Carson, 116.
[53] R. H. Gundry, *A Survey of the New Testament* (Grand Rapids: Zondervan, 1994) 256.

The glory of God was in the tabernacle in the wilderness, shining between the cherubim and in the pillar of fire and the cloud over the tent. Now "we have seen his glory, the glory of the One and Only, who came from the Father, full of grace and truth" (Jn. 1:14b). This glory was rooted in the goodness of God. When God's glory passed by Moses, God declared who He was. His nature was "compassionate and gracious...abounding in love and faithfulness."[54]

Therefore, in John's Gospel, logos also means divine self-revelation. God discloses Himself in and through Christ. When we see the goodness of Christ, we see the glory of God.

The Father and Son Relationship

As we noted earlier, the Logos was in a face-to-face relationship with God. He is God in the fullest sense of deity. (When was God ever without wisdom?) The relationship we call the Trinity is revealed in the prologue. This is a unique relationship, however, and John describes it wonderfully:

> The Word became flesh and made his dwelling among us. We have seen his glory, the glory of the One and Only, who came from the Father, full of grace and truth.—Jn. 1:14

> No one has ever seen God, but God the One and Only, who is at the Father's side, has made him known.—Jn. 1:18

The unique Son dwells eternally in an intimate relationship with the Father.[55] Although no one has seen God, the Word has been sent (or expressed) by the Father to reveal God to us. The Son is uniquely qualified to express God because He is "beside" God and Himself God. He is "the ultimate disclosure of God himself."[56]

Even Moses saw only the residue of God's glory as it passed by. He could never look directly into the face of God.[57] However, Christ took on flesh to reveal the glory of God. Burge noted, "Moses' request to see God was denied (Ex. 33:20; cf. Deut. 4:12); but Jesus has come to us from the very heart of the Father."[58]

The Father has bestowed upon the Son the "kind of glory a father grants to his *one and only, best-loved Son*[59]—and this 'father' is God himself. Thus it is nothing less than God's glory that John and his friends witnessed in the Word-made-flesh."[60]

Every word and deed of Christ demonstrated this glory. John records the heart of God expressed through Christ's love, faithfulness, holiness, miracles and so on. This is the glory that Christ reveals.

---

[54] Christ was also the Prophet like Moses (Jn. 6:14) who talked in a "face to face" way on Mount Sinai (Deut. 34:10).
[55] An intimacy perhaps portrayed in the actions of John who leaned upon the breast of Christ during the last supper (Jn. 13:23).
[56] Carson, 135
[57] See 1 Timothy 6:16.
[58] Elwell, 848.
[59] See D. Moody, *God's Only Son: The Translation of John 3:16 in the Revised Standard Version*, **Journal of Biblical Literature**, 1953, 213-219.
[60] Carson, 128.

When we follow Christ, then God is glorified, and we in turn receive of His glory (Jn. 17:10, 22). "This is to my Father's glory, that you bear much fruit, showing yourselves to be my disciples" (John 15:8).

The Connection between the Prologue and the Gospel

Several concepts from the Old Testament have merged together in John's prologue. John summarizes the Christ event, and establishes the themes he will explain in the rest of the gospel. D. A. Carson provides a useful list of verses that show the connection between the prologue and the rest of the Fourth Gospel. This list is reproduced below:

Topic/ Theme	Prologue	Gospel
the pre-existence of the Logos or Son	1:1-2	17:5
in him was life	1:4	5:26
life is light	1:4	8:12
light rejected by darkness	1:5	3:19
yet not quenched by it	1:5	12:35
light coming into the world	1:9	3:19; 12:46
Christ not received by his own	1:11	4:44
being born to God and not of flesh	1:13	3:6; 8:41-42
seeing his glory	1:14	12:41
the 'one and only' Son	1:14, 18	3:16
truth in Jesus Christ	1:17	14:6
no-one has seen God, except the one who comes from God's side	1:18	6:46

We have already discovered how the theme of the deity of Christ finds its roots in the prologue (Jn. 1:1-3, 18), as well as the overall apologetic purpose (Jn. 1:10-12). We can also find several of the other themes discussed in this workbook:

- The Trial Theme – Jn. 1:7-8, 15
- The Theme of the Father and Son Relationship – Jn. 1:18
- Theme of Faith – Jn. 1:12-13
- The Conflict Theme (Light/Darkness) – Jn. 1:5-9
- The Theme of Glory – Jn. 1:18
- The Theme of Life – Jn. 1:4

D. A. Carson summarizes:

> But supremely, the Prologue summarizes how the 'Word' which was with God in the very beginning came into the sphere of time, history, tangibility—in other words, how the Son of God was sent into the world to become the Jesus of history, so that the glory

and grace of God might be uniquely and perfectly disclosed. The rest of the book is nothing other than an expansion of this theme.[61]

Application

1. What kind of creative power do our words have?

2. Why was it necessary for Christ to come in the flesh?

3. Since Christ was at the side of the Father, what does that imply about what Christ revealed to us?

4. Since Christ is the Creator, how can He help us?

5. What is your view of the Creation? Do you agree with John that Christ is the origin of the creation of God (Rev. 3:14)?

6. Is it enough that Christ died for the world, or do we have to receive what He did (Jn. 1:11-12)? Explain.

7. Do unsaved family and close friends often receive what we have to say about Christianity? Why or why not? Do they often reject a relative's conversion experience? Explain.

---

[61] Op. cit., 111.

6

The Theme of the Holy Spirit

Bible Review

Read through the following verses. Pay careful attention to the titles, Person, and ministry of the Holy Spirit.

Key Scriptures

John 7:37-39
Key Thought _____

_____

Jn. 14:15-17, 26
Key Thought _____

_____

Jn. 15:26-27
Key Thought _____

_____

Jn. 16:7-18
Key Thought _____

_____

Jn. 20:21-22
Key Thought _____

_____

Comments and Analysis

1. What evidence is there in these verses that the Holy Spirit is a Person? What titles are given to the Holy Spirit in these verses?

2. What do these verses reveal to us about the trinity?

3. What do these verses tell us about the ministry of the Holy Spirit?

4. How is the life of God brought to mankind? What are the streams of life referring to? (See Jer. 17:13.)

5. Who gives the Holy Spirit? When was He given? How do we know that the Holy Spirit dwells within us? (See Acts 2; Ro. 8:16.)

6. How did Christ equip us as He sent us to continue His mission?

Review of the Holy Spirit in John's Gospel

Advocate for the Prosecution

We have already noted in Lesson #3 that the Holy Spirit is the Advocate for the prosecution. He is the one who convicts the world of sin, righteousness, and judgment (Jn. 15:18-16:11). He witnesses to unbelievers as we testify of Christ. Beasley-Murray affirms:

> Jesus is depicted as an intercessor *in* the court of heaven, representing the cause of his own, whereas the Holy Spirit is the Paraclete *from* heaven, supporting his own in the face of a hostile world.[62]

When Christ commissioned the disciples to continue His testimony to the world, He breathed on them to impart the Holy Spirit (Jn. 20:21-22). The Holy Spirit enables us to effectively continue Christ's ministry. This should give us great confidence in evangelism.

Just as it would be important for an Advocate of the Court to prepare a witness to give his or her testimony, so the Holy Spirit teaches us and reminds us about Christ's life and sayings. He "guides us into all truth" to help us give an accurate and effective testimony. He does this by speaking to our spirits (the "inner voice").[63] Gordon Chilvers writes:

> The place where the Holy Spirit witnesses is in our hearts. Hence it is called the inner witness or the secret witness. Being secret it cannot be shared or fully communicated to others. It is not something available to the checks of scientist or philosopher. Yet the witness is intensely real to us.[64]

Not only is there a general witness of God's will in our hearts, but the Holy Spirit also works prophetically in the lives of believers. He can reveal a "word of knowledge" or a "word of wisdom" or reveal the future to believers (1 Cor. 12-14).

The world does not understand or appreciate the ministry of the Holy Spirit. Nevertheless, those who have the Holy Spirit in them recognize the voice of the Good Shepherd and receive His teaching and guidance.

---

[62] G. R. Beasley-Murray, *Gospel of Life: Theology in the Fourth Gospel*, (Peabody: Hendrickson Publishers, 1991), 12.
[63] Is. 30:21; Ro. 8:16; 9:1; 1 Cor. 2:9-10; Gal. 4:6; Rev. 2:7, 11, 17, 29; 3:6, 13, 22.
[64] Gordon Chilvers, *The Internal Witness of the Spirit*, **Paraclete**, Summer 1971, 28.

Spirit of Truth

For His witness to be valid, the Holy Spirit must speak "the truth, the whole truth, and nothing but the truth."[65] John is careful to record for us that the Holy Spirit is the Spirit of Truth.

> And I will ask the Father, and he will give you another Counselor to be with you forever —the Spirit of truth. The world cannot accept him, because it neither sees him nor knows him. But you know him, for he lives with you and will be in you.—Jn. 14:16-17

> But when he, the Spirit of truth, comes, he will guide you into all truth. He will not speak on his own; he will speak only what he hears, and he will tell you what is yet to come. He will bring glory to me by taking from what is mine and making it known to you. All that belongs to the Father is mine. That is why I said the Spirit will take from what is mine and make it known to you.—Jn. 16:13-18[66]

The Spirit not only speaks truth, *He is truth*. In his first epistle, John declares, "And it is the Spirit who testifies, because the Spirit *is the truth*" (1 Jn. 5:6; see Jn. 14:6 of Christ). "As Defender of truth, He is therefore opposed to the 'spirit of error'"[67] (1 Jn. 4:6). Since He reminds disciples of what Christ did and said, the integrity of Scripture was guaranteed.

Streams of Living Water

Just as water is a necessary ingredient for life, so the Holy Spirit brings us "living water" to give us eternal life.[68] Just as water refreshes us, so the Holy Spirit also refreshes us spiritually and revives us emotionally. This life should spill out and overflow to others.

Jesus' words during the water-drawing ceremony of the Feast of Tabernacles (Jn. 7:37-39) were spoken to take advantage of the symbolism. "A procession led by a priest went down to the pool of Siloam, where a golden pitcher was filled with water, and returned to the temple as the morning sacrifice was being offered. The water was then poured into a funnel at the west side of the altar, and the temple choir began to sing the Great Hallel (Ps. 113-118)."[69] This was done to offer thanks for the gift of rain that God had provided and probably commemorated the miraculous waters provided at Meribah during the nation of Israel's wilderness journey (Nu. 20:2-13).

---

[65] Truth is an important theme in John's Gospel. It supports the trial theme and supports the testimony of the witnesses. Thomas D. Lea notes in *The Reliability of History in John's Gospel*, **Journal of the Evangelical Theological Society**, vol. 38, no. 3 (September 1995), page 400: "John uses *aletheia* [truth] twenty-five times, considerably more than any other gospel and more than any other NT book." The Holy Spirit's testimony is valid because He is speaking for Christ and bringing glory to Him, not to Himself.

[66] Although "spirit" is neuter gender, it should be noted that the Greek pronouns for "him" (autos and ekeinos) are used to refer to the Holy Spirit. Attributes of a Person are also applied to Him. He can be grieved (Eph. 4:30), lied to (Acts 5:1-4), resisted (Acts 7:51), and insulted (He. 10:29). You can quench the Spirit (1 Thess. 5:19), be led by Him, and He will guide believers into the Truth (Jn. 16:13).

[67] J. Oswald Sanders, *The Holy Spirit and His Gifts*, Grand Rapids: Zondervan, 1972) 31.

[68] See Prov. 4:23, 5:15; Is. 12:3, 55:1, 58:11; Jer. 17:13; Ezek. 47:1-11; Zech. 14:8; Jn. 4:14; Rev 22:1.

[69] Bruce, 101.

In a similar way, Christ was offering a greater gift of the Holy Spirit for those who come to Him in faith. The water drawn from the pool of Siloam speaks symbolically of Christ as the source of the true water. The water pouring out of the vessel was symbolic of the future outpouring of the Holy Spirit. Unlike the water rite that must be repeated year after year, the living water would stream up from the believer continuously. All of this was done for the praise and glory of God.

He Is the <u>Holy</u> Spirit

The Holy Spirit strives also to make us holy. He is called the *Holy* Spirit. He also teaches truth and wants to lead us into truth. Truth is the absence of falsehood and implies holiness and purity. The Holy Spirit is also called the "Spirit of burning" by Isaiah (Is. 4:4) and John the Baptist called the baptism of the Spirit a baptism of fire (Lk. 3:16). One of His most important ministries is to make us pure and righteous. He does this by convicting us when we sin.

Summary

Following F. F. Bruce's outline of John's Paraclete sayings,[70] the Holy Spirit is:

1. Helper - Jn. 14:15-17
2. Interpreter - Jn. 14:25-26
3. Witness - Jn. 15:26-27
4. Prosecutor - Jn. 16:4b-11
5. Revealer - Jn. 16:12-15

In all this, He is completely true and holy. His purpose is to glorify Christ (Jn. 16:14). His ministry to us is indispensable. He is our Advocate and Teacher who "abides forever."

---

[70] Bruce, pp. 301-302, 304-305, 315-316, 318, 320-321.

Application

1. What makes our testimony valid (cf. 1 Jn. 5:6-12)?

2. Does the Holy Spirit teach us truth from the Scriptures? How does He do this? By what authority is He able to do this?

3. How do I determine the will of God? Does the Holy Spirit guide us only through the Scriptures? Does He also guide us through speaking assurance of His will in our hearts? Do the Holy Spirit and the Word ever contradict each other? Explain.

4. Can the Holy Spirit guide us through prophecy? What checks and balances must be used?

5. Comment on the following: "Spiritual deafness is undoubtedly one of the greatest weaknesses of God's people today."[71] How do we open our ears to hear what the Spirit is saying?

---

[71] H. P. Jeter, *What is the Spirit's Role in Guidance?*, **Paraclete**, Summer 1976, 20.

Application

6. Describe an occasion where the Holy Spirit has spoken to you.

7. In what ways does the Holy Spirit empower us each day? (See, for example, John 14:27-29.)

8. Do you emphasize the gifts of the Spirit or holiness more? How do you balance gifts and character?

9. Is the mind important when the Holy Spirit communicates with us? (Note the *kind* of mind described in Ro. 8:7 and Ro. 12:2.)

10. How do we quench the Holy Spirit? How do you keep in step with the Spirit?

Themes in the Gospel of John

7

The Theme of Love

Bible Review

Read through the following verses. Pay careful attention to the way love was expressed in John's Gospel.

Key Scriptures

John 3:16
Key Thought _____

_____

John 11:33-36
Key Thought _____

_____

John 13:20-24
Key Thought _____

_____

John 13:34-35
Key Thought _____

_____

John 14:15, 21
Key Thought _____

_____

John 15:12-14
Key Thought _____

_____

John 21:15-17
Key Thought _____

_____

Comments and Analysis

1. What is the evidence of love? What did God do to show His love? Did Christ demonstrate the greatest kind of love? (See 1 Jn. 3:16.) What did Christ do for the disciples just before giving them the new commandment?

2. Is love conditional or unconditional? Is salvation conditional or unconditional? Explain.

3. Is love more a command we obey or a desire we feel? Is love more a matter of the will or a matter of the heart? Explain. (See 1 Jn. 5:2-3.)

4. What kind of love is described in these verses? What is the example and standard of this love?

5. Who was the disciple called "the disciple whom Jesus loved"? Did this disciple love Jesus greatly? Explain.

6. How was Peter admonished to show his love?

7. What happens when we love Jesus? What happens when we love each other?

Review of the Love Theme in John's Gospel

The previous verses only serve to underscore the importance of the topic of love to John.[72] In fact, many people refer to the Fourth Gospel as the "Gospel of Love." We have already noted the loving Father and Son relationship recorded by John. But there are several other expressions of love in John's gospel. Here are just a few.

God's Love for the World

Most people who have read John's Gospel recall the words of John 3:16:

> For God so loved the world that he gave his one and only Son, that whoever believes in him shall not perish but have eternal life.

This verse reveals so much about God's love. God loves a world of sinners. He loves them so much that He gave His unique Son—His special, well-beloved Son. His love is not just promises, but action. It is not just convenience, but sacrifice. It is the kind of action that costs Him dearly. The result of His love to us is eternal life—life that is fellowship in His eternal Love (Jn. 17:3). This was the greatest act of love, the greatest sacrifice of love, and the greatest gift of love.

No other verse so clearly declares that God's love is the reason and motive for the plan of salvation. Here the gospel message "is made unmistakably plain, in language which people of all races, cultures and times can grasp, and so effectively is it set forth in these words that many more, probably, have found the way of life through them than through any other biblical text."[73]

How is it that God should love us this much? C. S. Lewis commented:

> If it is maintained that anything so small as the Earth must, in any event, be too unimportant to merit the love of the Creator, we reply that no Christian ever supposed we did merit it. Christ did not die for men because they were intrinsically worth dying for, but because He is intrinsically love, and therefore loves infinitely.[74]

The love of God in Christ is the greatest invitation for the unbeliever to the gospel message. It makes perfect sense for John to emphasize the theme of God's love to encourage the readers to have faith in Jesus Christ. In fact, it is through our love of Christ that the Father's love reaches out to us:

> …the Father himself loves you because you have loved me and have believed that I came from God.—John 16:27

The crucifixion demonstrated above all else that God loves the world. The resurrection guarantees that this love has a future.

---

[72] The Greek noun *agape* (love) occurs seven times in the Fourth Gospel. The verb *agapao* occurs 34 times. The noun *philos* (affection) 6 times, the verb *phileo* 8 times. Agape is a common word for love, but when used of God's love, agape soars to new heights. For the subject in John's Gospel, see James Maoloney, *Love in the Gospel of John: An Exegetical, Theological, and Literary Study*, poublished by Baker Academic.

[73] Bruce, 90.

[74] Martindale and Root, 406. Extracts taken from C. S. Lewis, *Miracles*, (William Collins & Sons Ltd.).

Christ's Love for the Disciples

John not only emphasizes God's love for the world,[75] but also Christ's love and care for His disciples. Christ uniquely displayed this as He took a towel and basin of water and washed the disciple's feet (Jn. 13:1-17)—even the feet of the one who would betray Him! This passage records that by His example of service (both here and prophetically of the crucifixion), Christ loved His own "to the full extent" (NIV) or "to the end" (eis telos).

After finishing, Christ pointedly asks, "Do you understand what I have done for you?" Then explains, "You call me 'Teacher' and 'Lord,' and rightly so, for that is what I am. Now that I, your Lord and Teacher, have washed your feet, you also should wash one another's feet. I have set you an example that you should do as I have done for you" (Jn. 13:12-15). These debriefings were critical for the training of the disciples. Not only was Christ's love powerfully demonstrated, but it was also sealed to their hearts by the explanation of the Master Teacher.

Christ loved them as His disciples, but also as His friends. One way He showed this was by sharing with them His relationship with the Father. He declared: "I no longer call you servants, because a servant does not know his master's business. Instead, I have called you friends, for everything that I learned from my Father I have made known to you" (Jn. 15:15).

Christ revealed His deep friendship feelings in many ways. For instance, the tears Christ shed at the tomb of Lazarus revealed His tender friendship. Many of the Jews that were there were prompted to declare, "See how he loved him!" (Jn. 11:36). In John 17, Jesus demonstrated this kind of love by His impassioned prayer for His friends.

Finally, to His "friends" He showed His greatest love by laying down His life. "Greater love has no one than this, that he lay down his life for his friends" (John 15:13). Here is genuine love indeed! A Good Shepherd lays down his life for the sheep (Jn. 10:11-15)—even if those disciples as "stray sheep" misunderstand, betray and deny Him. Love must be demonstrated in action. And true friendship is based on sacrifice. In contrast, a hireling has failed friendships because such relationships are not grounded in commitment and sacrifice.

Christ's love as a friend is offered as a benefit to those who become His disciples. This friendship benefit fits very well with John's overall apologetic purpose. Showing the love that Christ has for believers encourages those who are unsaved to enter the kingdom and partake of His love. It is as if John says, "Don't you want to share this love and be His friend too?"

This shared love is clearly stated in John 14:20-21:

> On that day you will realize that I am in my Father, and you are in me, and I am in you. Whoever has my commands and obeys them, he is the one who loves me. He who loves me will be loved by my Father, and I too will love him and show myself to him.

This is an invitation into the inner "circle of divine love"[76] expressed between the Father and the Son. What greater fulfillment of love can be desired?

---

[75]What other gospel writers call love for enemies (Mt. 5:43-47).
[76]Bruce, 304.

Love for One Another

Just as the love expressed to the world draws unbelievers to God, and just as the love expressed by Christ to His friends invites them, so the love believers have for one another should draw others to God. Jesus said:

> A new command I give you: Love one another. As I have loved you, so you must love one another. By this all men will know that you are my disciples, if you love one another.—John 13:34-35

It was not new to love one another. The Bible says in Leviticus, "Do not seek revenge or bear a grudge against one of your people, but love your neighbor as yourself. I am the LORD" (Lev. 19:8). However, the standard of love in this Old Testament verse is the way you would want to be treated yourself. Christ pointed to a new standard—the example shown in Himself! *"As I have loved you,* so you must love one another." No other standard will do. Beasley-Murray contrasted these two commands:

> The old command was part of the old covenant; this command is the law of the new covenant. As the commands of the Mosaic Law were given to Israel as their part in the covenant by which they became God's people, so the "new command" is the obligation of the people of the new covenant in response to the redemption of Christ. It is the *standard* of love, however, which makes the new command distinctive: *"as I have loved you."* Love of self is a powerful instinct, but it cannot rise to the heights of the divine love for humankind revealed in the cross of Christ; and the noblest self-regarding love cannot compare with the outflow of love from the Redeemer who draws his own to him.[77]

When the love of a believer emulates the standard of Christ's love, it becomes the distinguishing mark of the believer. It is Christ's love that sets us apart from all others and makes us uniquely His disciples. "By this all men will know that you are my disciples, if you love one another" (Jn. 13:35).

This kind of love results in servanthood. It is "compassion in action." The following are the words of Mother Teresa:

> It's not how much we give, but how much love we put in the *doing*—that's compassion in action...All God really wants is for us to love Him. The way we can show our love for Him is to serve others...My message to the people of today is simple. We must love one another as God loves each one of us.

When compassion takes action, then the world sees Christ in us. However, it is not just the love *of* God in us that motivates us to service, but it is also the love *for* God that causes us to serve. For all believers who have the revelation of servanthood understand that when they give a cup of cold water to a needy person, they give it to Christ.

---

[77]Beasley-Murray, 111.

Two other specific demonstrations of love are worth noting in John's gospel.

John's Love for Jesus

One cannot read the Gospel of John without recognizing the love John had for his Lord. John leaned upon Christ during the emotional struggles of the last supper (Jn. 13:18-30). He followed Christ at a distance after His arrest (Jn. 18:15-16). John stood at the foot of the cross while Christ placed Mary into his care (Jn. 19:26-27). He ran to the sepulcher with Peter after Mary Magdalene's report. Here he saw the empty tomb and believed (Jn. 20:1-9). Even when Jesus took Peter aside to correct him, John followed behind, probably wanting the companionship of Christ (Jn. 21:20).

John refers to himself as "the disciple whom Jesus loved" (Jn. 13:23; 19:26; 20:2; 21:7, 20). Christ had a special fondness for John. John's portrayal of Christ and his insights into the Father and Son relationship reveal a deep respect and intimate love between Christ and John.

Peter's Love for Jesus

John 21:15-18 records a unique interview with Peter. Christ challenges Peter's love for Him three times and re-commissions Peter to pastoral care. Although much attention has been given to the interchange between the two Greek words for love (agapao and phileo), these may have been used simply for variety.[78] What is often missed and is most important is the charge to Peter to show his love by action! Feeding (nurturing, teaching, and caring) the sheep would demonstrate that Peter was obeying Christ and fulfilling the standard of love.

Obedience and love are inseparable. Jesus said, "If you love me, you will obey what I command" (John 14:15). Both commitment and conduct equaling that commitment are essential for Christ-like love.

---

[78]Scholars disagree on the significance. Note Bruce's comments, 404-405.

Application

1. What does eternal life imply about God's love? How can you wash someone's feet (figuratively speaking)?

2. Comment on the following: "The more we recognize the depth of our sin, the more we recognize the love of our Savior."[79]

3. Is it difficult to serve someone you know to be a Judas? Explain.

4. Read John 13:3. Comment on how knowing the things in this verse helps you serve others.

5. Can churches remain racially divided and still fulfill John 13:34-35? Can we be reconciled and worship separately?

6. Comment on the following: "Christ-like love should be the hallmark of the church."[80]

---

[79]Carson, 484.
[80]Burge, 870.

Application

7. Jesus asked Peter if he loved Him three times in John 21. What did Jesus expect Peter to do to show His sincere love?

8. Do we love as others love us or as Christ loved us? Can we love God and not love one another? (See 1 Jn. 4:11-21.) Comment on the following: Love is serving others compassionately.

9. What are the two moral absolutes (Deut. 6:4-5; Lev. 19:18; Mt. 22:36-40; Jn. 13:34-35; Gal. 5:13-14)? Comment on the following: Laws and commands in Scripture are nothing more than restatements of the two moral absolutes.

8
The Theme of Glory

Bible Review

Read through the following verses. Pay careful attention to John's use of glory.

Key Scriptures

John 1:14
Key Thought _____

_____

John 2:11
Key Thought _____

_____

John 8:50, 54
Key Thought _____

_____

John 12:27-28
Key Thought _____

_____

Jn. 13:31-32
Key Thought _____

_____

John 15:8
Key Thought _____

_____

John 17:4-5
Key Thought _____

_____

Comments and Analysis

1. Do the Father and Son share the same glory? Explain.

2. How did Christ reveal His glory? What was the miracle at Cana in Galilee?

3. What was the hour of Christ's glorification? What was the heart cry of the Son during His hour of glory? What was the response of the Father?

4. Did Christ seek glory for himself? How did Christ bring glory to God? What must we do to bring glory to God?

5. What is our chief purpose in life?

Review of the Theme of Glory

In a previous lesson we already mentioned the importance of the theme of glory in John's gospel. We saw in Exodus 33:18-22 that God's glory is particularly rooted in His goodness. When God's goodness is revealed to the world, this is His immanence or glory. Glory is the majestic goodness of God bursting forth as overwhelming "light" into the natural realm.[81]

Though Christ shared the glory of the Father intrinsically and eternally,[82] John shows us the glory of the incarnated Son (Jn. 1:14, 18). Jesus could display His dazzling glory (the transfiguration, Mt. 17:2; Mk. 9:2[83]) but John wants us to see the glory of Jesus in the goodness of His character, words, and deeds. Christ's miracles, for instance, reveal His glory. After Christ turned water into wine for a wedding, John records, "This, the first of his miraculous signs, Jesus performed at Cana in Galilee. He thus *revealed his glory*, and his disciples put their faith in him (Jn. 2:11).[84]

Christ also brought glory to God by completing His task (Jn. 17:4)—"the way of the cross," which is the greatest expression of the goodness and glory of God. Christ lifts up His voice on the cross to proclaim that His work is *finished*. Ajith Fernando writes:

> The word *glory* is used when the nature and character of God has been manifested in its splendor. And that is what happened at the cross. We saw the full expression of his holiness and love, which forms the essence of His nature. His holiness was manifested in his hatred for sin that caused him to punish it so severely. His love was manifested in his giving his Son to die in our stead.[85]

Restated, the glory of God is revealed by what Christ did and said—uniquely and supremely in Christ's death, burial, and resurrection (Jn. 7:39; 12:27f.; 13:31f.; 17:1, 5). We see this also in the double meaning of "lifting up" (Jn. 3:14; 8:28; 12:32). It represents both the greatest moment for the triumph of darkness in the cruelty of the cross, yet also the supreme means of exaltation of Christ (Jn. 13:31-32) when, having completed His mission, He returns to the glory He had with the Father. David Hill points out:

> The Father is glorified in the sacrificial death of Jesus because this event marks the completion of the work committed to the Son (Jn. 17:4; 19:30) and represents total obedience to the Father's will. Throughout his entire ministry Jesus glorified the Father: but death sets the seal on his obedience and self-dedication and therefore supremely glorifies the Father, and at the same time, leads to the reception by Jesus of his heavenly glory; 'Father, glorify thou me in thy own presence with the glory which I had with thee before the world was made' (Jn. 17:5).[86]

---

[81] In a lesser way, such was the residue of light that still remained on the face of Moses when he came down from meeting God on the mount (Ex. 34:29-35).
[82] The glory Isaiah saw was the glory of the Son (Jn. 12:41; 17:4-5, 24).
[83] Jesus possessed this glory continually but not openly.
[84] See also Jn. 11:4, 40.
[85] Ajith Fernando, *The Supremacy of Christ* (Wheaton: Crossway Books, 1995), 152.
[86] David Hill, *The Request of Zebedee's Sons and the Johannine* δοξα-*Theme*, **New Testament Studies**, 13, 281-285.

Christ, like a grain of wheat that must die before it bears fruit, gives us the fruit of life only after His death (Jn. 12:24). In turn, we glorify God when we bear much fruit (Jn. 15:8). This can only be accomplished when we die to self and follow Christ as obedient disciples. Mark notes that when James and John desired to share Christ's glory, the Lord asked them if they were able to share in His suffering. "Can you drink the cup I drink or be baptized with the baptism I am baptized with?" (Mark 10:39). There can be no glory without suffering for Christ.

Christ thus modeled the way of the cross for us—the process of self-denial and glory. He stood for truth and willingly submitted to trial and torment. He was elevated on the cross in humiliation and extreme suffering—but also in exaltation (Jn. 3:14; 8:28; 12:32-34). His crucifixion and resurrection ultimately glorified God by bringing justification and salvation to those who believe. The Father in turn glorified the Son (Jn. 8:54; 11:4), and the Son in turn shared His glory with His disciples (Jn. 17:10, 22).[87]

This process is illustrated below:

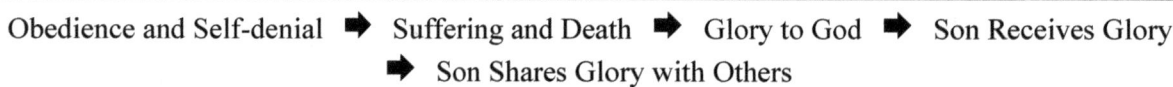

Obedience and Self-denial ➡ Suffering and Death ➡ Glory to God ➡ Son Receives Glory ➡ Son Shares Glory with Others

This process can be summarized as: 1) Self-glory denied; 2) Sacrifice and suffering experienced; 3) Glory given to God; 4) Glory received from God; 5) Glory shared with others.

If we follow Christ in the way of the cross (taking up our cross daily), then God is glorified in our lives. Paul affirmed this when he remarked that if we suffer with Him, we share in His glory (Ro. 8:17). This process sanctifies us (Jn. 17:17-19). God honors us and places His glory in us (by the presence and filling of the Holy Spirit). In turn, others see this glory in us and desire to partake of it. Again, the apostle Paul put it this way:

> Therefore we do not lose heart. Though outwardly we are wasting away, yet inwardly we are being renewed day by day. For our light and momentary troubles are achieving for us an eternal glory that far outweighs them all.[88]—2 Corinthians 4:16-17

Lastly, unity and community are formed as a result of this process. These in turn become a testimony to the world that God is in the Church. "I have given them the glory that you gave me, that they may be one as we are one: I in them and you in me. May they be brought to complete unity to let the world know that you sent me and have loved them even as you have loved me" (Jn. 17:22-23).

---

[87] Though God does not share the glory and honor due Him alone (Is. 42:8), He does honor us and cause His glory to *reside in us* by the Holy Spirit.

[88] "When Paul speaks of 'an eternal weight of glory' (2 Cor. 4:17), he is recalling the etymology of the Hebrew word (which is derived from the root kbd, whose primary meaning is 'to be heavy')." B. Metzger and M. Coogan, editors, *The Oxford Companion to the Bible* (New York: Oxford University Press, 1993), 254.

Summary

As we noted in a previous lesson, several expositors recognize two literary divisions in John's Gospel. The first division, chapters 1-12, has to do with Jesus' public ministry: the discourses, teaching, and events showing the supremacy of Christ—especially His signs. In fact, these chapters are also called "The Book of Signs." Gary Burge explains:

> Chapters 1-12 is called the "Book of Signs," since it records Jesus' numerous revelatory miracles...Note how the hymn at the beginning is almost an overture, a curtain-raiser to the drama, which really begins at 1:19. This is followed by a unit centered on John the Baptist...The story moves quickly from scene to scene: a miracle at Cana; cleansing the temple; Nicodemus...The final reference to John the Baptist (10:40-42) refers back to the beginning of the entire sequence of signs (1:19 and following), making another closing frame and reiterating the value of Jesus' signs.[89]

The second division, chapters 13-21, involves the activities and teachings during the Passover and the events of Christ's passion. It "is called 'The Book of Glory,' since on the cross Jesus is glorified (13:31)."[90]

When we look at the overall structure in John's Gospel, we can readily see that glory plays a vital role in John's message. In the Book of Signs, Jesus discloses the glory of God and brings glory to God publicly through His miracle-signs. Some, as John the Baptist, are sign posts that Jesus is the Messiah. Even the feasts are sign-festivals pointing to Christ who is their greater fulfillment. In the Book of Glory, Jesus brings the ultimate glory to God by completing His redemptive mission through the suffering of the cross. In a very real sense, John's Gospel is all a Book of Glory.[91]

---

[89] Burge, *Interpreting*, 76, 79.
[90] Op. Cit., 76.
[91] For more information about the structure of John's Gospel, see Appendix C, *The Structure of John's Gospel*.

Application

1. Does the countenance of someone who has been in the presence of God reflect God's glory? Explain.

2. Can we skip over any of the steps in "the way of the cross?" Explain.

3. Will the Father affirm us during our times of agony and glory? Are obedience to God's will and a desire to glorify Him necessary prerequisites to His help?

4. How does God give joy in the midst of suffering (Jn. 17:13-16)?

5. How can an hour of agony become an hour of glory?

6. Comment on the following: "Christians must remember that the fruit that issues out of their obedient faith-union with Christ lies at the heart of how Jesus brings glory to the Father."[92]

7. Comment on the following statement by Martin Luther: "Affliction is the best book in my library."

---
[92] Carson, 518.

Application

8. How does the world recognize disciples of Christ (Mt. 7:20)? How effective has the Church been in showing Christ? Explain.

9. Is there a lack of unity in the Church? Why or why not?

10. How was Lazarus' sickness to glorify God (Jn. 11:4)?

11. How did Christ's miracles affect His creation?

9

The Theme of Life

Bible Review

Read through the following verses. Pay careful attention to John's use of life.

Key Scriptures

John 1:4
Key Thought _____
_____

John 3:16-17
Key Thought _____
_____

John 3:36
Key Thought _____
_____

John 5:24
Key Thought _____
_____

John 5:26
Key Thought _____
_____

John 6:32-35, 51-58
Key Thought _____
_____

Key Scriptures (Continued)

The thief comes only to steal and kill and destroy; I have come that they may have life, and have it to the full.—John 10:10

Jesus said to her, "I am the resurrection and the life. He who believes in me will live, even though he dies; and whoever lives and believes in me will never die. Do you believe this?"—John 11:25-26

Now this is eternal life: that they may know you, the only true God, and Jesus Christ, whom you have sent.—John 17:3

But these are written that you may believe that Jesus is the Christ, the Son of God, and that by believing you may have life in his name.—John 20:31

Comments and Analysis

1. More than anything else, what does John want the readers of his gospel to have? How much life does he want us to have?

2. What does life mean in John's gospel? Does life mean living forever? Does it mean a relationship with God?

3. Is material wealth included in the concept of life? Explain.

4. What does John mean when he says that believers have "crossed over from death to life?" Explain the connection between life and resurrection.

5. What must we do to acquire life?

6. Why is life "in his name?" Can life be through any other name?

Review of John's Use of the Theme of Life

Life Is in Christ

You probably remember the story of the death of Lazarus, one of Jesus' dear friends (Jn. 11). When Christ heard the news that Lazarus was sick, he tarried two days before going to see him. After he arrived, Jesus learned that Lazarus had already "been in the tomb for four days" (Jn. 11:17). Martha met him with both regret and hope:

> "Lord," Martha said to Jesus, "if you had been here, my brother would not have died. But I know that even now God will give you whatever you ask."

Jesus replied confidently, "Your brother will rise again." Whatever Christ's intentions were in delaying to come, He was now determined to perform an incredible miracle.

But Martha still had trouble seeing what Christ meant. She answered, "I know he will rise again in the resurrection at the last day." Until the final trumpet call, death will come to us all. But death is no final barrier for Christ. His reply contains the most hope-filled words in the New Testament: "I am the resurrection and the life" (Jn. 11:25). Life and resurrection are not just some force that Christ commands, they are intrinsically in the *Person* of Christ (Jn. 5:26). He is the source of life.

D. A. Carson noted:

> "Jesus' concern is to divert Martha's focus from an abstract belief in what takes place on the last day, to a personalized belief in him who alone can provide it...There is neither resurrection nor eternal life outside of him."[93]

Christ backed up His words with the resurrection of Lazarus. The miracle gave proof that Jesus is who He said He was—the source of life. And He is the only source of life, for He said, "No one comes to the Father except through me (Jn. 14:6).[94]

Christ gives life to all those who hear His words and believe (Jn. 1:4; 5:21-24). At the resurrection of the dead, all will hear His voice and rise to be judged. Anyone who has believed in Christ "will not be condemned; he has crossed over from death to life" (Jn. 5:24).

---

[93] Carson, 412.
[94] Access to life is only through the gate to the sheepfold. This gate is Christ (Jn. 10:9-10).

Life through Relationship

Christ declared, "I have come that they may have life, and have it to the full" (Jn. 10:10). But what kind of life is this? Unfortunately, what is often defined as "abundant life" today, i.e., "materialism,"[95] is nowhere approved by Jesus. He did not say, "I have come to give you material wealth, and material wealth more abundantly."[96] In John's gospel, life means having an eternal relationship with God. Ajith Fernando comments:

> By describing this as "life...to the full" He is contrasting the life that He gives with all other ways of life. Those others all fall short of the fullness that only the One who created us can give. This is what Francis of Assisi (1182-1226) found out. He was the son of a wealthy cloth merchant. After Francis' spiritual awakening in his twenties, his father was convinced that he was insane and denounced him. Francis took on a lifestyle of poverty. But he did not miss the riches he gave up. He said, "To him who tastes God, all the sweetness of the world will be but bitterness." Jesus explained this same kind of fulfillment saying, "I am the bread of life. He who comes to me will never go hungry, and he who believes in me will never be thirsty" (John 6:35). After we come to Him, healthy ambition and restlessness is not lost. That would make life boring. In fact, we have a new thirst for God, for His glory and for His ways. But the world's hunger that takes away our joy and peace is gone for good.[97]

John recorded the following definition of life: "That they may know you, the only true God, and Jesus Christ, whom you have sent" (John 17:3). Life is knowing Christ. The more we intimately know Him, the more we partake of life.

We have already noted that God's love is a sacrificial one. Our relationship is anchored securely in Christ because we know that He will not fail us. The hired hand flees the flock when the wolf attacks, but the Good Shepherd is not like that. He knows His sheep and is willing to lay down His life for them (Jn. 10:14-15). Life is, therefore, the result of all that Christ gives to us in our relationship with Him. Life is the "fulfillment of a love-relationship with God."[98]

Life may include His leading us like sheep to good pasture (Jn. 10:9), but life does not mean giving us the "American dream."

---

[95] By "materialism" I mean an inordinate desire for and interest in wealth; greed. It is often seen as an expectancy for God to give us everything we want, whether we need it or not. It is often disguised in the Church today as "faith." The result of this thinking is that Christians who are not wealthy are not exercising "faith." Nothing is farther from the truth.

[96] When the synoptic writers recorded Christ's promise that believers would receive manifold in this life (Mt. 19:39; Mk. 10:30; Lk. 18:30), He was not referring to materialism, but rather that Christians share all things in common as brethren.

[97] Fernando, 175.

[98] Op. cit., 175.

Life Is Possessed Now

Life is not just a future phenomenon, but something we enjoy when we receive Christ. Life is something that we can possess now because we possess the relationship now. Beasley-Murray comments:

> Now there is a major difference between the concept of "life" in the Fourth Gospel and that in the Old Testament, early Jewish literature, and the synoptic Gospels: in all these latter writings "life" or "eternal life" is a future hope, since it is life in the kingdom of God that is to come; in the Fourth Gospel, however, it is characteristically the gift of God given in the present time.

By having a relationship with Christ, we immediately enjoy the life that is in Him. By partaking of His "flesh and blood" (Jn. 6:51-58; e.g., believing in His passion and resurrection), we immediately receive the spiritual life afforded by his vicarious atonement. The emblems of the Lord's Supper represent this very truth, and act as visual reminders of our present life in Him.

Further, our future eternal life is the ultimate consequence and assurance of knowing and believing in Christ now. In a very real sense then, eschatology (the study of end time events) is Christology (the study of Christ)! Christ is the past, present, and future of all life. He is intrinsically the "resurrection and the life" (Jn. 11:25).[99]

Summary

What does this life from Christ do for us? It causes us to "cross over" from death into life—the whole realm of the kingdom of God. It rescues us from judgment. It guarantees our resurrection. It places the Holy Spirit into our hearts and brings us into immediate, intimate fellowship with God. It provides us "pasture" and safety. It gives us the light of truth and causes us to know Christ. For those who receive His life, it "restores, renews, and fulfills the life given to humanity in creation."[100] Finally, it glorifies God, and thus fulfills our eternal purpose.

How does the theme of life fit with the other themes in John's Gospel? Tenney answers this:

> To believe that Jesus is the Christ (Messiah) and the Son of God involves the total acceptance of the revelation of God that he offers, the acknowledgment of his divine authority, and the fulfillment of the commission he entrusted to his disciples. The total scope of this belief is illustrated in the narrative of this Gospel. Its result is eternal life, a new and enduring experience of God by the believer. This conclusion ties together the three persistent themes of the Gospel: the "signs" that demonstrate Christ's nature and power; the response of "belief" that is exemplified in the crises and growth in the lives of the disciples; and the new "life" that is found in the relationship with Christ.[101]

---

[99] This is declared forcefully in the book of revelation when only the Lamb can break the seals and unleash the events of the last days (Rev. 5ff).
[100] Beasley-Murray, 11.
[101] Tenney, 196-197.

Application

1. Explain how the apostle Paul described life in Philippians 1:21 and 2 Corinthians 5:17. How does this compare to John's description of life?

2. In John 10:9, Jesus says, "I am the gate; whoever enters through me will be saved. He will come in and go out, and find pasture." Is this a promise of meeting our needs? Explain.

3. What is your response to Christ's question in John 11:26: "Do you believe this?" Have you received His life?

4. What guarantee of eternal life do we have as a result of the resurrection of Lazarus and the resurrection of Jesus? (See Jn. 14:19 and 1 Jn. 3:14.)

5. How do we not see death (Jn. 8:51) if our mortal life comes to an end?

6. How can John 17:3 be the basis of unity in the Church?

Application

7. What correlations do you see between John 10 and Psalm 23?

8. In what way does the theme of life illustrate the supremacy of Christ?

9. Comment on the following: "The central purpose [of] Jesus [is] to glorify the Father by imparting life to men."[102] (See John 11:40-42.)

10. How does God's pruning help us have God's abundant life (Jn. 15)?

---

[102] Op. Cit., 162.

10

Themes in the Nicodemus Discourse

Bible Review

Read through the Nicodemus discourse (Jn. 3:1-21). As you read, note any of the themes we have studied (listed below) and record your thoughts below.

Notes on Themes

1. Overall Purpose

2. Deity of Christ

3. Father/Son Relationship

4. Trial (Testimonies)

5. Conflicts

6. Love

7. Glory

8. Life

Review of the Nicodemus Discourse

Nicodemus has learned of the reputation of Christ as a miracle worker. He sincerely wanted to investigate the man from Galilee further. This religious leader's curiosity led him to meet the Master, but the night meeting may have been designed for caution, perhaps even to conceal his association with the radical Teacher. After all, hadn't Christ just cleansed the temple (Jn. 2:13-25)? A Pharisee and member of the ruling class could not be too careful.[103]

Nicodemus opened the conversation: "Rabbi, we know you are a teacher who has come from God. For no one could perform the miraculous signs you are doing if God were not with him."

As Christ did so often, his response went directly to the heart of the matter: "I tell you the truth, no one can see the kingdom of God unless he is born again." The words "born again" probably bear a double meaning. One must be born spiritually, "of the water and the Spirit,"[104] and one must be "born from above," where Christ has gone and returns (v. 13, 31). The kingdom is of heaven, not of this earth.

Nicodemus, like so many of us, looked only at Christ's words from a temporal, worldly perspective. To this failure, Christ offered a natural to spiritual comparison. The wind has an effect on nature but we cannot see it. This is like those born of the Spirit—their new lives are totally affected by the Spirit but we cannot see the cause.[105] Christ is the master teacher here. Often, spiritual things must be explained in concrete, physical terms.

However, Nicodemus is still confused, so Christ explains His comparison: "I have spoken to you of earthly things and you do not believe; how then will you believe if I speak of heavenly things?" (v. 12). All of this is wrapped up in a mild rebuke of Nicodemus. Spiritual leaders must have spiritual insight. (Nicodemus will partially redeem himself as he later defends Christ (Jn. 7:50) and openly "joins Joseph of Arimathea in burying and anointing the body of Christ"[106] after His passion (Jn. 19:39).)

So that there could be no confusion, Jesus declared His supremacy and mission forthrightly: "No one has ever gone into heaven except the one who came from heaven—the Son of Man." Christ identifies Himself as the Messiah—God who has taken on human flesh to reveal the Father.

To guide Nicodemus further, Christ used an Old Testament illustration sure to be familiar to Him: "Just as Moses lifted up the snake in the desert, so the Son of Man must be lifted up, that everyone who believes in him may have eternal life." The Israelites in the wilderness had spoken against God. Their rebellion resulted in a plague of venomous snakes that killed many. Through Moses' intercession, God made a way of deliverance from the plague. Those who looked at the snake that Moses lifted in the wilderness were healed from the bites (Num. 21:4-9).

The principle is the same with Christ. Those who believe on the One who was lifted on the cross shall be saved eternally. Just as the Israelites could not deliver themselves from the deadly serpents, so we cannot save ourselves from judgment to come. We need the sacrifice of Christ.

---

[103] Nicodemus may have been a secret disciple like Joseph of Arimathea (John 19:37-38).
[104] This is probably a reference to the new beginning promised in Ezek. 36:25-26: "I will sprinkle clean water on you, and you will be clean; I will cleanse you from all your impurities and from all your idols. I will give you a new heart and put a new spirit in you..."
[105] Wind is also likened to the Spirit in Scripture (Job 7:7; Is. 40:31; Ezek. 37:9-10), especially if we equate this with the breath of God.
[106] Burge, 851.

In the heart of Nicodemus, as in many readers, was the question of Christ's authority. Could He be the Son of God? Not only is this an actual discussion with Nicodemus, but it is an occasion best suited for John's apologetic purpose. By recording this meeting with Nicodemus, John has just given *the reader* another confirming testimony of what Christ has done.

By cleansing the temple, Christ was establishing Himself as supreme over the Temple, the most important religious place to the Jews. By showing us Christ's vastly superior spiritual understanding compared to Nicodemus, John has sealed Christ's supremacy over the religious establishment.

After the discourse with Nicodemus (vs. 1-15), John goes into an extended commentary on the final words of the discourse: *eternal life*. In the rest of the chapter, John sums up the mission, judgment, and verdict of Christ, and the conflicts that His light brings to the world. Gary Burge notes:

> Belief in the Son gains eternal life (vv. 15, 16, 18). Disbelief gains judgment and condemnation (vv. 18, 19, 35). This sums up the worldview characteristic of John's Gospel: one is either attracted to or repulsed by the light (vv. 19-21); one either pursues truth or evil. There is no equivocation here. Yet the coming of the Son was not inspired by a desire to condemn—it stemmed from love (v. 16). But judgment was an inevitable result. Light brings exposure (v. 20): it reveals who we really are.[107]

---
[107] Op. cit.

Application

1. What teaching techniques did Christ use? How can these help us to reach others for Christ?

2. Comment on the following: Christ has a way of cutting to the root of the matter and not allowing us to dwell on the past.

3. What did Nicodemus do right? What did he do wrong? How can spiritual leaders learn from this? What makes a spiritual leader?

4. What can we do to maintain a spiritual perspective?

5. Nicodemus was looking for a natural, national kingdom. What kind of kingdom did Christ offer? What were the entrance requirements? Is knowing the Bible enough to be saved? Explain.

6. Does being "born again" or "being born from above" have anything to do with reincarnation? Explain.

7. What do we find in this passage that causes us to worship Christ? Comment on the supremacy of Christ.

11

Themes in the Samaritan Woman Discourse

Bible Review

Read through the Samaritan Woman discourse (Jn. 4:1-42). As you read, note any of the themes we have studied (see the list below) and record your thoughts.

Notes on Themes

1. Overall Purpose

2. Deity of Christ

3. Father/Son Relationship

4. Trial (Testimonies)

5. Conflicts

6. Love

7. Glory

8. Life

Review of the Samaritan Woman Discourse

Christ was on His way to Galilee to avoid any premature conflicts with the religious authorities who were growing concerned with His popularity. This trip took Him through Samaria, whose inhabitants were not always respected by the Jews. Samaritans were the progeny of inter-marriage with non-Jewish inhabitants and held to a syncretistic religion. Some Jews took a different route to by-pass Samaria altogether. Jesus was not afraid of this racial hatred, however, and confronted it head on.[108]

"The well of Jacob lies at the foot of Mount Gerizim, the center of Samaritan worship."[109] The "sixth hour" (vs. 6) was not the usual time for women to draw water from the well. This was a very hot time of the day, around noon. Perhaps this woman's reputation did not permit her to come to the well with the other women, who may have shunned her. In any case, she was alone when she met Christ and was surprised that He asked her for a drink. F. F. Bruce explains:

> The Evangelist's explanation of her surprise—another of his typical parenthesis—is not simply that (as the older versions have it) "Jews have no dealings with the Samaritans" but more specifically that (as the NEB renders it) "Jews and Samaritans, it should be noted, do not use vessels in common". If the woman complied with Jesus' request, he would have had to drink from her vessel, since he had none of his own. This would have involved a risk of ceremonial pollution for a Jew even if the owner of the vessel had been a male Samaritan, but the fact that the owner was a woman made that risk a certainty, from the standpoint of a strictly observant Jew. No wonder that Jesus' request astonished the woman; by asking such a favor from her he had shown most unexpected goodwill.[110]

Her reply was argumentative and reflected the bitterness of the racial and religious prejudice: "You are a Jew and I am a Samaritan woman. How can you ask me for a drink?" (vs. 9). As always, Christ got right to the heart of the matter: "If you knew the gift of God and who it is that asks you for a drink, you would have asked him and he would have given you living water." Christ used the natural need for water to point to the spiritual need of life found in Himself. The Holy Spirit brings spiritual life to every believer when He indwells us. This is the "gift" that Christ could give her.[111]

The woman still did not perceive the significance of Christ's statement, so Christ explained further. "Everyone who drinks this water will be thirsty again, but whoever drinks the water I give him will never thirst. Indeed, the water I give him will become in him a spring of water welling up to eternal life." Her spiritual condition was what Christ was most concerned about. What He has to offer is of eternal value and does not need replenishing.

The spiritual meaning was still beyond the grasp of the Samaritan woman, so Christ tried another approach: He told her to call her husband. Tenney comments:

> Jesus' request to call her husband was both proper and strategic—proper because it was not regarded as good etiquette for a woman to talk with a man unless her husband were present; strategic because it placed her in a dilemma from which she could not free

---

[108] See Luke 10:29-37.
[109] Tenney, 54.
[110] Bruce, 103.
[111] Christ used the "Living water" symbolism again at the water ceremony of the Feast of Dedication in John 7:37-39. Here John clearly explained that the living water is the Holy Spirit. See Ps. 42:1; Is. 55:1; Jer. 2:13; 17:13; Zech. 13:1.

herself without admitting her need. She had no husband she could call, and she would not want to confess her sexual irregularities to a stranger. The abruptness of her reply shows that she was at last emotionally touched.[112]

Christ was penetrating her conscience and probably making her uncomfortable. She admitted that He was a prophet[113] to know such things, but then tried to side step the issue with another comment on the differences between Jews and Samaritans. Moses had set up an altar on Mount Gerizim when the Israelites entered the Promised Land (Deut. 27:1-28:68). This was now where the Samaritans worshipped. But true worship of God is far more spiritual than a place of worship, no matter how sacred, and Christ is supreme over any sacred place.

Jesus directed her attention to the nature of the Father and the resultant requirement of worship: "Believe me, woman, a time is coming when you will worship the Father neither on this mountain nor in Jerusalem...Yet a time is coming and has now come when the true worshipers will worship the Father in spirit and truth, for they are the kind of worshipers the Father seeks. God is spirit, and his worshipers must worship in spirit and in truth" (vs. 21, 23-24).[114]

At this point the Samaritan woman seemed to allow that the argument will one day be settled by the Messiah. To this Jesus gives the definitive reply: "I who speak to you am he" (vs. 26). Imagine her excitement! The village outcast was the first one to meet the Messiah. She hurried off to tell the rest of the village and forgot her water pot behind. "The wellspring of perennial refreshment was now bubbling up within her."[115]

While she scurried off, the disciples returned. When the disciples offer Him food, He replies, "I have food to eat that you know nothing about...My food...is to do the will of him who sent me and to finish his work" (vs. 32, 34). Jesus used an object lesson and took advantage of the "teachable moment." There is a harvest of souls that must be reaped and Christ finds spiritual nourishment (life) by fulfilling the Father's will to save the lost. Just as we need bread and water to survive in the natural, so we need spiritual bread and water to live in the spiritual.

When the villagers flocked to see Jesus, they bore witness that He was indeed the Messiah.

What a challenge this must have been to the readers of John's Gospel! Here were the disrespected Samaritans, and the least of them—a Samaritan adulteress—and all of them received Christ and believed. What a remarkable contrast this is to the doubt of the Pharisees! The Samaritans bore witness that this "is the Savior of the world."

---

[112] Op. cit., 55.
[113] Burge, page 852, notes that the titles of Christ improve from "Sir" (vs. 11, 14); "Prophet" (vs. 19), "Christ" (vs. 25, 29), to "Savior of the world" (vs. 42).
[114] The nature of God is described in three other passages in the New Testament: "God is a consuming fire" (He. 12:29), "God is Light" (1 Jn. 1:5), and "God is Love" (1 Jn. 4:8, 16).
[115] Bruce, 112.

Application

1. Did Christ recognize differences of race? How did Christ confront racism? Was the manner in which Christ confronted racism an example of how we should confront it? Is there anyone to whom it could be said that you have no dealings with them?

2. Was Christ distracted by the racial comments of the woman from Samaria? Did Christ always control the conversation? Did He always lead the conversation to the important matters? How does this influence the way we evangelize the lost?

3. Christ turned a casual meeting into an evangelistic opportunity. What must we do to be ready for such "divine appointments?"

4. How did Christ use the natural to explain the spiritual? How can we use this teaching tool in evangelism?

5. Comment on the following: Christ "was more interested in winning the woman than in winning an argument."[116]

---

[116] Tenney, 54-55.

Application

6. Nicodemus was from the upper class; the Samaritan woman was from the lower class. Did Christ show any partiality to either because of class distinctions? Is Christ's acceptance of the Samaritan woman an example for us today? Explain.

7. The Samaritan woman thought that Christ was going to give her something to make her life easier. Does Christ offer us a life of ease? What does He offer?

8. What supernatural revelation did Christ use in His witnessing? Should we exercise the gift of the Word of Knowledge in a similar way?

9. Should we remind people of their sins? Explain.

10. Does the fact that Christ talked to this woman with no one else around give men the right to counsel women alone? Explain.

11. How does the Holy Spirit help us worship the Father?

12

Themes in the Man Born Blind Discourse

Bible Review

Read through the Man Born Blind discourse (John 9:35-41). As you read, note any of the themes we have studied (see list below) and record your thoughts below.

Notes on Themes

1. Overall Purpose

2. Deity of Christ

3. Father/Son Relationship

4. Trial (Testimonies)

5. Conflicts

6. Love

7. Glory

8. Life

Introduction to the Discourse with the Man Born Blind

Healing the Man Born Blind

One Sabbath day Christ spit on the ground, mixed dirt and saliva as a poultice[117], put it on the eyes of a blind man, and sent him off to wash in the Pool of Siloam.[118] He must have stumbled as he groped and hurried on his way. Can you imagine the burst of colors as he washed his face and opened his eyes? For the first time he could see the water, sky, buildings, plants, and people! Remember, he was not just *restored* to sight, he was healed of *congenital* blindness—the man was born blind. He had never seen what we take for granted. I wonder how long he paused to take it all in.

When the man came home his family and neighbors were amazed. This was an extraordinary miracle! When they learned it was Jesus who had healed him, they wanted to know where he was. But the blind man had never seen Christ, he had only heard his voice and felt his compassionate touch. So they took him to the Pharisees.

Unfortunately, healing on the Sabbath (and perhaps the making of clay as well) was contrary to the rabbinical Sabbath work restrictions. The Pharisees immediately attacked Jesus for violating their laws. Isn't it characteristic of religious people to react like this when their authority is challenged? One wonders who was really blind.

Nevertheless, the miracle holds up under the closest of scrutiny and the blind man refuses to deny Christ even under two interrogations. He remained steadfast, showing remarkable savvy and courage, chiding them: "I have told you already and you did not listen. Why do you want to hear it again? Do you want to become his disciples, too?" (vs. 27). "Their incessant questioning exhausted his patience, and he indulged in some sarcasm by insinuating that their repeated inquiries showed an interest in becoming disciples of Jesus."[119] This response so infuriated the Pharisees that they delivered a torrent of insults. When he argued that God would not listen to Christ if He were a sinner, they were so enraged that they excommunicated him on the spot (vs. 34), "thus isolating him from his family and friends and debarring him from employment."[120]

Gary Burge adds the following insightful remarks:

> It is interesting to trace the attitudes of the blind man and the Pharisees here. The former makes three confessions of ignorance (vv. 12, 25, 36) but in the end is led to true vision and faith (vv. 34-38). The latter make numerous confident statements of knowledge (vv. 16, 24, 29) but are shown to be ignorant (v. 41). The story is symbolic then of spiritual vision and blindness complete with their attendant dispositions (cf. the similar blindness motif in Mark 8:14-30).[121]

Andrew Lincoln has pointed to the contrast in this discourse between the man born blind, who moves steadily toward light and truth, and the religious authorities who move more and more into darkness. The man born blind recognizes Jesus as the man who healed him (v. 11), a prophet (v.

---

[117] Carson, 363-364, notes, "Not a few church Fathers saw an allusion to Genesis 2:7: since God made human beings out of the dust of the ground, Jesus, in an act of creation, used a little dust to make eyes that were otherwise lacking."
[118] Carson, 365, notes that the Jews rejected the waters of Shiloah in Isaiah 8:6 and here reject Christ.
[119] Tenney, 104.
[120] Tenney, 105.
[121] Burge, *Evangelical Commentary*, 859-860.

17), then becomes Jesus' disciple (v. 27), recognizes that Jesus is from God (v. 33), that he is Lord and Son of Man (v. 38), and then he finally worships Jesus (v. 38b).

The religious authorities move from a divided verdict about Jesus (9:16) to unbelief (v. 18-19), to a verdict that Jesus is a sinner (v. 24), and then to excommunicating the man born blind (v. 34). Here again is the irony of John. The one who was blind, now sees; the ones who could see became blind. The verdict of the court of heaven is apparent.

Throughout this event, it was only Jesus who understood what was really important. When Christ and the disciples first encountered the blind man, the disciples wanted to know who sinned to cause the blindness.[122] The Pharisees wanted to know who had the insolence to heal on the Sabbath. The disciples were concerned with blaming someone and the Pharisees didn't want their authority challenged! Even the blind man's parents were more concerned for their own welfare and didn't really support their son for fear of the Pharisees. The only one who had compassion on this man was Christ. The important thing was neither judging others, keeping religious rules, nor protecting ourselves—it was helping someone. Isn't this the real meaning of the Sabbath?

Jesus' reply to the disciple's initial question is important: "Neither this man nor his parents sinned...but this happened so that the work of God might be displayed in his life" (Jn. 9:3).[123] Suffering happens in a fallen world. It is not for us to find fault or lay blame, but to counteract the affects of the Fall. This is the work of God. When this happens, God is glorified.

In the midst of this incident, Christ had claimed to be "the Light of the World" (Jn. 9:5).[124] Christ proved His claim by healing the man born blind. As he did then, He continues to open the eyes of the blind—both naturally and spiritually.

The Supremacy of Christ

By healing the blind man, Christ demonstrated His supremacy:

1. Over the physical body.

2. Over the Sabbath day.[125]

    Christ pointed out elsewhere, "The Sabbath was made for man, not man for the Sabbath. So the Son of Man is Lord even of the Sabbath" (Mk. 2:27-28).[126]

3. Over the Jewish festival of Tabernacles, which is a special Sabbath.

    This festival of water and light appears in Chapter 7:1-52 and provides the setting for the healing in Chapter 9. Jesus commanded the blind man to wash the mud and saliva in the

---

[122] Some rabbis evidently believed that the unborn child could sin in the womb.
[123] See Jn. 5:17, 6:38, and 11:9.
[124] See also John 8:12.
[125] See also John 5.
[126] Man's restrictions hardly portray the true spirit of the fourth commandment. The basis of the law was to love God and love one another. The Sabbath work restrictions, although intended to help apply the law to everyday life, actually made the law of none effect. The Sabbath commandment was never intended to cause us to stop loving one another (in this case by healing). Here is a clear case of where tradition had counteracted the truth of God's Word.

Pool of Siloam, "the source for the water ceremonies at Tabernacles."[127] Not only is Christ the true source of the (living) water of the feast (vs. 37-39) but also the source of its light. Gary Burge notes:

> As in the previous section, the festival is mentioned and its primary symbols described. Jesus then replaces the symbol or demonstrates his own authority over its meaning. At Tabernacles, when the temple was sponsoring water and light ceremonies, Jesus stands in the temple and announces that he is "living water" and "the light of the world."[128]

The Discourse of the Man Born Blind is a wonderful example written "that you may believe that Jesus is the Christ, the Son of God, and that by believing you may have life in his name" (Jn. 20:31).

Summary

In contrast to the spiritual blindness of the Pharisees, the once-blind man progressively grew in faith, the light dawning and then shining out with determination from his heart.[129]

The once-blind man became a worshipper and disciple of the Light of the World. At the beginning of the chapter, this man was blind both naturally and spiritually. When he was given natural sight, he came to also see the Light of Life. Others could see naturally, but refused to come to the Light because their deeds were evil. The former received forgiveness, the latter had their guilt remain.

---

[127] Burge, *Evangelical Commentary*, 860.
[128] Burge, *Interpreting*, 77.
[129] Burge, page 860, notes: "In much the same way that the Samaritan woman in John 4 witnessed her faith developing through a progression of titles for Christ, so here the narrative parades Christ's names ("Jesus," v. 11; "Siloam," v. 11; "prophet," v. 17; "Christ," v. 23; "from God," v. 33; "Son of Man," v. 35; "Lord," v. 38)."

Application

1. Is suffering always the result of our own sin? (See Job; Gal. 4:13; 2 Cor. 12:7.) Is it our fate to suffer for our parent's sins (Ex. 34:7)? Is bad behavior always punished? Explain.

2. Is a miraculous sign always evidence of God at work? (See Deut. 13:1-5.) Are the signs and miracles of Jesus compelling evidence that He is the Christ? Explain.

3. How did the neighbors, parents, religious leaders, and the man born blind react differently to the miracle? What really motivated the Pharisees?

4. Do Christians receive persecution for their testimony of Christ? Explain.

5. Did the Light penetrate everyone's heart in this story? What prevented it from penetrating all the hearts? Is anything keeping the Light from penetrating your heart?

Application

6. Are we always aware of our needs? Are we always aware of the solution to our problems? Explain.

7. What did Christ show us about the importance of follow-up?

Appendix A
Locating the Belief/Unbelief Conflict

The following table illustrates the locations of belief and unbelief in the Fourth Gospel:

Chapter	Location	Belief/Unbelief
Ch. 1	Bethabara beyond Jordan (vs. 28)	Belief
Ch. 2	Cana of Galilee (vs. 1) - (Capernaum (vs. 12))	Belief
	Jerusalem (vs. 13, 23)	Unbelief/Belief
Ch. 3	Jerusalem	Unbelief
	Judea (vs. 22)	Belief
Ch. 4	Samaria (vs. 4)	Belief
	Cana of Galilee (vs. 43, 45)	Belief
	(Nazareth (vs. 44) cf. Lk. 4:14-32)	Unbelief
Ch. 5	Jerusalem (vs. 1)	Belief/Unbelief
Ch. 6	Galilee (vs. 1)	Belief/Unbelief
Ch. 7-9	Galilee (vs. 1) - (Unbelief in Judea)	Belief/Unbelief
	Jerusalem (vs. 3, 11)	
Ch. 10	Jerusalem	Belief/Unbelief
	Bethabara (vs. 40)	Belief
Ch. 11	Bethany (vs. 1, 20)	Belief
	Jerusalem (vs. 10-11)	Unbelief
	Jerusalem (vs. 12)	Belief/Unbelief
Ch. 13-20	Jerusalem	Belief/Unbelief
Ch. 21	Galilee (vs. 1)	Belief

Appendix B
Belief/Unbelief Conflict in John's Gospel

The following table illustrates the conflict between belief and unbelief in John's Gospel:

Conflict	Belief and/or Unbelief	Scripture
Faith Established	"Through Him all men might believe."	Jn. 1:7
Light Dawns	Belief of John the Baptist	1:15, 29-34
	Belief of the Disciples	1:35-51
	Belief of Mary	2:3-5
1st Conflict	Unbelief of the Jews (Temple Hierarchy)	2:18-20
		2:22
	Belief of Disciples	2:23
	Belief of Mary	3:2, 4, 9, 12
	Belief and Unbelief of Nicodemus	3:14-36
	Faith and Unbelief Explained	
Light Breaks Forth	Belief of the Woman at the Well	4:1-29
	Belief of the Samaritans	4:30, 39-42
	Belief of the Nobleman and Household	4:43-54
	Belief of the Invalid (?)	5:1-9
2nd Conflict	Unbelief of the Jews	5:10-13, 15-16, 18
	Faith and Unbelief Explained	5:19-47
3rd Conflict	Belief of the Multitudes	6:2, 14
	Unbelief of the Multitudes	6:30-31, 41-42, 52
Darkness Intensifies	Faith Explained	6:29, 33, 35-40, 44-51, 53-58
4th Conflict	Unbelief of the Disciples	6:60, 64, 66, 70-71
Light Continues	Belief of the Disciples	6:67-69
5th Conflict	Unbelief of the Jews	7:1
6th Conflict	Unbelief of His Own Brethren	7:2-5
	Belief of the People	7:31, 40-41
7th Conflict	Unbelief of the Pharisees	7:32, 48, 52
8th Conflict	Unbelief of the People	7:41-44
9th Conflict	Unbelief of the Pharisees	8:13, 19, 22, 25
	Belief of Many	8:30
10th Conflict	Unbelief of Many	8:33, 39, 44-46, 48, 52-53, 57, 59
	Faith of the Blind Man (?)	9:1-7, 17, 31-33, 35-38
11th Conflict	Unbelief of the Pharisees	9:16-24, 26, 29, 34
12th Conflict	Belief and Unbelief of the Jews	10:19-21, 24-26, 31, 33, 39
Darkness and Light Growing	Faith Explained	10:37-38
	Belief of Many	10:42

Conflict	Belief and/or Unbelief	Scripture
Light Climaxing	Faith of Martha	Jn. 11:22, 27
	Faith of Mary	11:32
	Belief of Many	11:45
13th Conflict	Unbelief of Some	11:46
	Unbelief of Pharisees	11:47-54, 57
	Belief of Many	12:9-11
	Unbelief Explained	12:37-47
	Many Leaders Believe	12:42
	Faith Explained	12:44-50
	Faith Encouraged	ch. 13 - ch. 17
14th Conflict, Darkness Climaxing	Unbelief of Soldiers and Officials, Judas	18:3
15th Conflict	Unbelief of the High Priest	18:19-24
16th Conflict	Unbelief of Pilate	18:38, 19:1, 9
17th Conflict	Unbelief of the Soldiers	19:2-3
	Faith of Joseph of Arimathaea	19:38
Victory of Light	Faith of Mary	20:16
	Faith of the Disciples	20:19-20, 25
18th Conflict	Unbelief of Thomas	20:24
	Faith of Thomas	20:27-28
	Faith Explained	20:29-21:25

Appendix C
The Structure of John's Gospel

John's purpose forms a framework for interpreting his gospel. The various parts of the gospel, including the prologue, events, discourses, movements between narratives, and the explanatory notes of John,[130] all work together to support John's theme.

John is no different than the Synoptic authors in presenting the historical account of Jesus along with their unique purpose and perspective. "Each Evangelist presents theology along with history and 'interprets' Jesus for readers."[131] John takes from his own resources those pieces of Christ's life that are necessary to prove his theme. These are sewn together to show His deity and bring the reader to Life in Christ. The result is a unity that defies attempts to dispute Johannine authorship or break up John's Gospel into various sources.[132]

The literary structure of John can present some puzzles for us, however, but they can be resolved with careful examination. Gary Burge notes, for example, the "literary seams" in the gospel. "In these instances the chronological, topical, or dramatic flow of the narrative appears disjointed."[133]

One example is the sequence of John 5 and 6. Burge comments,

> Jesus moves abruptly from Samaria to Galilee to Jerusalem back to Galilee again and back once more to Jerusalem, without transitions...Compare this with what we gain just by reversing the order of chapters 5 and 6. Now 6:1 makes chronological sense because Jesus finishes a miracle in Galilee at the close of chapter 4. Jesus then moves from the west bank of the sea to the east bank.[134]

I personally believe that John was concerned with the theme first and then with the historical events. He chooses only those that were necessary for his purpose. If their chronological arrangement seems a bit "choppy" or even out of order, it is because the events must serve his purpose. Burge cites D. A. Carson that "moving the chapters would destroy a thematic unity they share as they stand."[135] Tearing apart the gospel with form or source criticism "neglects the overall literary and theological unity of John and makes the 'garment serve the seams' rather than the other way around."[136]

A small comparison between the book of Jeremiah and John's Gospel may provide some insights into the arrangements of books. The prophecies of Jeremiah are arranged according to genre first, then by chronology. If one reads the book expecting prophecies in chronological order, one

---

[130] The explanatory notes are what Merrill C. Tenney called, "the footnotes" in John's gospel. See Merrill C. Tenney, *The Footnotes of John's Gospel*, Bibliotheca Sacra, Oct. 1960, 350-363.
[131] Gary M. Burge, *Interpreting the Gospel of John* (Grand Rapids: Baker Book House, 1992), 26. I am indebted to Burge's work for the bulk of this appendix.
[132] Gary Burge gives an excellent account of the internal and external evidence of Johannine authorship in Chapter 2.
[133] Op. cit., 62. Mr. Burge lists several of these on pages 63-66.
[134] Op. cit., 64.
[135] Op. cit.
[136] Op. cit., 68.

would become lost almost immediately. The book must be read by grouping the prophecies according to their literary type, then by connecting them historically. Some prophecies are woes, some are legal, some are comforting, and so on. Similarly, John's book must be read according to its own thematic coherence and "to examine its final message (instead of traces of its development)."[137]

Gary Burge gives a very plausible break down of the form of the final story on pages 75 to 82 and pages 101 to 107 of his book. Burge sees two major divisions. Chapters 1 through 12 of John's Gospel cover Jesus' public ministry, chapters 13 through 21 cover Jesus' personal glorification. The first part is often called the "Book of Signs," and the second part is often called the "Book of Glory." This is illustrated below:

Prologue Ch. 1:1-18	Jesus' Public Ministry "Book of Signs" Ch. 1-12	Jesus' Personal Glorification "Book of Glory" Ch. 13-20	Epilogue Ch. 21

> Chapter 12 seems a clear climax to the public ministry: it sums up Jesus' efforts, cries in despair over disbelief, and reaffirms the divine origins of Jesus' words. John 13:1 switches the scene to Passover, remarks that Jesus is now departing from the world, and narrows the stage to those who have followed him.[138]

These sections are further broken down and outlined by Burge. He notes the "internal signals" that divide the literary units.

> Episodes in Cana (the first and second miracles) frame the section on Jewish institutions. The festivals are named, because in each scene Jesus does something to exploit a symbol of that festival in his teaching (Sabbath-work, Passover-bread, Tabernacles-water and light, Dedication-Jesus' consecration).[139]

> The Book of Glory is dominated by the events of the upper room and the passion account. From chapters 13-17 Jesus is center stage, preparing his disciples for his death.[140]

Burge concludes that the "John we possess has a careful, intentional organization."[141] "Clearly the text of John is made up of sources pieced together to form a unified narrative. If we look carefully we can discern seams where these sources have been stitched together...Each theme is knit into the larger fabric and when we pause to stand back, the garment we call the Fourth Gospel takes on a striking and wonderful quality."[142]

Burge also makes several useful comments to the structure of John's gospel by explaining the macro and micro contexts of the book. The macro context has been dealt with above. The micro context of John 10 is explained on pages 106 through 107 as an example of interpretation. In

---

[137] Op. cit., 75.
[138] Op. cit., 76.
[139] Op. cit., 77-79.
[140] Op. cit., 80.
[141] Op. cit., 79.
[142] Op. cit., 82.

each segment of the chapter Jesus reveals "something about His identity, first through the festival metaphor and then abstractly...After each revelation there is a response."[143] Here again John is using the events to draw the reader to salvation—to receive who the Christ really is. John invites us to respond to Christ by identifying with the response of others. This is a wonderful literary device that works with John's apologetic purpose. The doubt of the reader follows the doubt of the crowds. The reader can easily identify with the confusion of the disciples. The dawning of the truth in Peter and John is the same awakening the Holy Spirit brings to the reader. The hands of the reader reach into the side of Christ along with Thomas and the reader exclaims with him, "My Lord and my God!" This is the structure of John's Gospel, and this is John, the writer, at his best.

---

[143] Op. cit., 107.

Appendix D
Christ as the Faithful and True Witness

When I consider the subject of being a faithful witness, I am reminded of a very good friend of mine who as a young man fell in with the El Quintos gang in New York City. He and four other gang members were "hanging out" on the streets one night looking for trouble. They decided to break into a closed liquor store to get some booze. In a nearby alley, they kicked in a store window and took several bottles. A few minutes later two officers stopped and arrested them, confiscated the liquor, and took them to the police station. For five grueling hours the police interrogated them. They convinced the young men that they would be released if they would confess to the break-in and to a mugging that had occurred the same night, not far from where they were. Finally giving in, they signed the papers, but then learned that they had confessed to a homicide! Convicted as a teenager of a crime he never committed, my friend grew up in a New York prison. I met him years later after his release. He had responded to an altar call at our church and had given his heart to the Lord. His early life serves as a tragic reminder of the affects of sin, especially false testimony.

A peculiar condemnation lies at the feet of a society that dupes young people into lying about a crime just for the convenience of clearing the legal docket. But everywhere we find false testimony—among corporate executives who deny complicity to "cooking the books" to college students plagiarizing material off the Internet. Indeed, lying is rapidly becoming a cultural norm.

Legal Testimony within the Mosaic Covenant

Fallen humanity's predisposition for lying demonstrates society's need for laws to deter and punish false testimony. In fact the finger-of-God-inscribed Decalogue, which underlies Western Civilization's system of jurisprudence, specifically forbids us from "bearing false witness;"[144] and the Mosaic Law proscribed severe penalties for those bearing falsehood, depending on the nature of the case. For example, anyone found bearing false testimony received the penalty intended for the accused (Deut. 19:18).[145] Additionally, Deuteronomy requires the valid testimony of two or more witnesses,[146] especially for cases involving capital crimes (Deut. 17:6-7; Nu. 35:30). Such provisions spring from the character of God, who exists as absolute Truth, and who abhors every falsehood and exposes each one.[147]

However, bearing honest testimony before a legal assembly constitutes only a portion of the broad scope of the legal testimony/witness setting of the Mosaic Covenant. The civil legalities surrounding testimony fall within the much greater purview of the court of heaven. Psalm 82, for

---

[144] Ex. 20:16; 31:18; Deut. 5:20; 9:10; cf. Ex. 23:1.
[145] Additionally, if someone has pertinent testimony, but withholds it from the judicial investigation, that person is held accountable and must present a sin offering (Lev. 5:1).
[146] Deut. 19:15; cf. Jn. 8:17; Lk. 9:5; cf. Mt 18:16; 2 Cor 13:1; 1 Tim 5:19. We all know the application of this requirement at Christ's trial before the Sanhedrin, where the witnesses could not agree concerning Christ's remarks about dismantling and rebuilding the temple (Mk. 14:55-59; cf. Jn. 2:18-22).
[147] Ps. 31:5; Is. 65:16; Prov. 6:17, 19; Jn. 14:17; 16:13; 1 Cor. 4:5; Eph. 5:11; 1 Jn. 4:6.

instance, depicts earthly judges[148] as representatives of heaven who should administer justice impartially (c.f. Deut. 1:17; 2 Chron. 19:4-7). However, this psalm indicts them for their failure to do so, and Asaph, the psalm's composer, presents testimony against the judges before the "Great Assembly" (presumably the Divine Court, Ps. 82:1-5).

Even the Decalogue itself and the Deuteronomic covenant terms with Yahweh form a "testimony" for or against the nation of Israel, depending on their compliance with the terms (Ex. 16:34; 25:16ff; 30:18). Since the Ark of the Covenant held the tablets of stone, with the Book of the Law placed beside the Ark (Ex. 40:20; Deut. 31:26), Moses termed both the Ark and the tabernacle places of "Testimony"—the Ark of Testimony and the Tabernacle of Testimony respectively (Ex. 26:33-34; Nu. 1:53).[149] Since the tabernacle was the meeting place between God and His people, the articles of testimony were thus "deposited before the Lord" (in the same manner as Samuel's updates to the covenant in 1 Sa. 10:25). This illustrates the close relationship of the nation to heaven, especially regarding legal/covenant matters.

When Joshua renewed the Mosaic Covenant at Shechem (Josh. 24; cf. Deut. 31:9-13), he warned the Israelites against future infidelity and about the severe consequences if they turned from God. At their insistence to remain under God's covenant obligations, Joshua proclaimed them to be *witnesses* of God (Josh. 24:22). Joshua then updated the covenant record and set up a final witness stone as a reminder (Josh. 24:27) of their covenant relationship with God.

Prophets as Witnesses

In large part the prophets proclaimed the testimony of God as His representatives (Ex. 4:10-16; 7:1; Micah 3:8; Zech. 7:12). Jeremiah insisted that the source of the true prophet's message was the Council of the Lord (Jer. 23:18; cf. Amos 3:8 and 1 Kings 22). No wonder, then, that the prophets often introduced their proclamations with "Thus says the Lord" or other similar phrases.[150]

Several important Old Testament prophets participated in the proceedings of the Divine Court and there received their commission as messengers of God to deliver the judgments of the court.[151] They frequently brought lawsuits from the Divine Court to Israel[152] or

---

[148] On the use of "elohim" for judges, see Ex. 22:28 and S. Lewis Johnson, *The Old Testament in the New* (Grand Rapids: Zondervan, 1980) 29.

[149] Likewise, he named the tabernacle "the Tent of Meeting" as it existed as the meeting place between God and Israel. Thus, it provided a place for the judgment of sin by sacrifice and for knowing the will of God (Ex. 28:30).

[150] See also 2 Sa. 23:2 and Mk. 12:36.

[151] Is. 41:27; Jer. 23:18; Is. 3:13-15, 25-26; 6:8; 41:27; Ezek. 2-3 (especially 2:9-3:1); Amos 3:7; Hag. 1:13; Mal. 3:1; Rev. 4:1; 11:3-12; 22:18-19.

[152] Is. 1:2-3, 18-20; 3:13-15, 25-26; Lam. 3:58; Ho. 3:3-17; 4:1-19; Amos 3:1; Micah 6:1-5. Sometimes called "complaint speech" (Hebrew *rîb*). According to James Limburg, the verb occurs in the prophets in Is. 3:13; Micah 6:1; Hos. 2:4, 4:4; and Jer. 2:9. The noun occurs in Micah 6:2; Hos. 4:1, 4:4; 12:3; Jer. 25:31. In the majority of Old Testament examples, "the subject of the verb is an aggrieved party making an accusation against an aggrieving party." James Limburg, *The Root Rib and the Prophetic Lawsuit Speeches*, **Journal of Biblical Literature** 88, Sept. 1969, 297. See also the discussion in Leon Morris, *The Biblical Doctrine of Judgement* (Grand Rapids: Eerdmans, 1960) 38-40. See also Rev. 6:10. A prophet's authority rested squarely on knowing the will of the court and in the confidence that God would back up His decisions (Is. 44:26). As a side note, sometimes prophets glimpse into the spiritual realm to view the delivery of the court edicts. Such were the examples of Zechariah and the "flying scroll" of judgment (Zech. 5:1-4), and the letters to the seven churches of Revelation 2-3. Each document contained "testimony" for or against the parties addressed.

challenged the Israelites to argue their case before the Divine Court.[153] Thus, these prophets were "witnesses" bearing heaven's edicts to the people.[154]

During the later years of Samuel's ministry, for example, the prophet assembled the tribes at Gilgal to confirm Saul as king of the new monarchy (1 Sa. 11:12-12:25). Following the offerings and celebration, the scene took on courtroom overtones and turned somber as Samuel presented God's lawsuit against them. Samuel first challenged the Israelites to find any fault with himself—to "testify" against him in the presence of witnesses (1 Sa. 12:3a). After the people responded that no violation could be found, Samuel had the people approach the "bar of God's justice"[155] and hear His accusation against them. They were about to learn that they had sinned by demanding a king, for until that time the Lord had been their king (1 Sa. 12:12).

Amos 3:1-2 and 9-15 exemplifies the lawsuit process. The passage both begins and ends the lawsuit[156] with God's warning against the nation of Israel: "I will call you to account for your iniquities." The lawsuit shows a court convening with a call for witnesses (vs. 1, 9), the Judge's speech (vs. 2, 10),[157] the indictment (vs. 2, 11), and the sentence (vs. 11-15).[158]

Amos also cites his credentials as a court witness who speaks with heaven's authority: God "does nothing without revealing his plan to his servants the prophets" (vs. 7). He then commands the court witnesses to, "Hear this and testify against the house of Jacob" (vs. 13). Amos concludes with a promise of restoration for the remnant (Amos 3:12).

As a witness of the court of heaven, the prophets often found themselves in opposition to a recalcitrant nation. Often the people placed great pressures on the prophets to yield to the popular perspective, leading the prophets to lament their adversity.[159] In contrast, God often admonished or encouraged the prophets to remain faithful to their testimony (c.f., Jer. 1:17-19; 20; 28; 38).

We should not move on from this Old Testament summary without adding a short note concerning prophets in the New Testament. The concept that prophets testify for the Divine Court comes together in Revelation where John acts as a commissioned prophet and court recorder.[160] A voice from heaven instructs him to eat the testimony scroll and then prophesy "about many peoples, nations, languages and kings" (Rev. 10:11). It is no wonder, then, that Scripture refers to the Book of Revelation as *prophecy*[161] and as the *testimony* of Christ.[162] The

---

[153] Is. 41:21-23; 43:26; see also Job 19:25; Jer. 12:1; Prov. 23:10-11.
[154] 1 Kings 22:19-23; Is. 6:8-13; Jer. 23:16, 18; Acts 10:42-43; Rev. 19:10.
[155] Ronald Youngblood, *1 Samuel*, in Frank Gaebelein, general editor, *The Expositor's Bible Commentary*, vol. 3 (Grand Rapids: Zondervan, 1986) 646.
[156] This forms an inclusio surrounding God's lawsuit.
[157] Marjorie Boyle cites Huffmon that the Hebrew word *yada* of Amos 3:2 was used "as a technical term for recognition of the treaty stipulations as binding." See Marjorie Boyle, *The Covenant Lawsuit of the Prophet Amos: III 1 – IV 13*, **Vetus Testamentum** 21 (July 1971), 344.
[158] See L. Sinclair, *The Courtroom Motif in the Book of Amos*, **Journal of Biblical Literature** 85, Sept. 1966, 350-353.
[159] See Elijah in 1 Kings 19:1-18, who resisted the pressures, and Balaam in Numbers 22:4-41, who gave in to the pressures.
[160] The court convenes in Rev. 4-5; 9:13; and 20. Revelation records judgments throughout the book.
[161] Rev. 19:10; 22:7, 10, 18-19.
[162] Rev. 1:2, 9; 12:17; 19:10 (2x); 20:4.

two ideas are synonymous when seen as part of heavenly courtroom drama. "For the testimony of Jesus is the spirit of prophecy" (Rev. 19:10).

God as Witness

That God also plays the role of witness in this covenant jurisprudence should not surprise us.[163] He sees all that happens and watches over His covenant to keep its requirements and bring justice and judgment to the nation (2 Chron. 16:9). For example, Isaiah brought Yahweh's lawsuit against the nation (Is. 3:13ff). On this occasion the Lord takes His place in court to judge the nation and bases His judgment on His own testimony regarding oppression and haughtiness.[164]

However, as sovereign over all, God's testimony reaches beyond the Mosaic covenant to encompass a cosmic trial where heaven weighs *all* nations in the balance. Though the heavenly courtroom ministry functions within the covenant administration, God's providential law touches all. Micah, for one, shows us that God's judgment against Israel becomes a witness against all the nations. They, also, will not escape His righteous judgment (Mic. 1:2-7).

The Lord's testimony is the truth evaluation regarding all things. (Christ reminds us that God's testimony is far more dependable than that of any human's [Jn. 5:33-36].) It is based on His righteous nature and equitable decisions. From this vantage point, the whole of Scripture serves as God's testimony, as it is the written Word of God (Mk. 7:13; He. 4:12) revealing His justice and judgments.

Christ as the Faithful and True Witness

In view of this background, we can understand how Christ fulfills the role of messenger *par excellence* for the Divine Court. He is *the Prophet* who was sent from heaven with the testimony of God the Judge (Deut. 18:18-19; Jn. 8:12-18, 50; cf. Mal. 3:1-5).[165] During His earthly ministry Christ spoke as a prophet keenly aware of His connection to heaven—in many cases using the courtroom language of "witness" and "testimony" (Jn. 3:31b-32; 5:31-47; 8:14, 17-18).[166]

Christ demonstrated this connection to heaven through His intimate fellowship with the Father. For instance, the words that the Father gave, the Son gave to others (Jn. 7:16-17; 8:40, 47; 12:49-50). As the Father worked, so did the Son (Jn. 5:17-19). Furthermore, *the Son spoke what He has seen in the Father's presence* (Jn. 8:38). Conversely, the Father always heard the Son (Jn. 11:42). Christ declared, "For I have come down from heaven not to do my will but to do the will of him who sent me" (Jn. 6:38). Thus, Christ was heaven's perfect *Witness*.

---

[163] Ge. 31:50; Judges 11:10; 1 Sa. 12:5; 20:23; Jer. 29:23; 42:5; Micah 1:2; Jn. 8:14, 17-18; Acts 14:3, 17; 1 Jn. 5:10.

[164] A common practice when making an agreement between two parties was to cite the Lord as a witness (Ge. 31:50; 1 Sa. 20:23, 42; Mal. 2:14). In addition, when leaders of the nation declare that heaven and earth (or a natural object, such as a rock or altar of stones) bore witness, they most likely represent the fact that God witnesses the events (Ge. 31:44-54; Josh. 22:10ff).

[165] See Mt. 13:57; Lk. 13:33; Jn. 4:19; 6:14; 7:40; 9:17; He. 1:1-2. For an excellent summary of Christ as the Prophet, see TDNT, vol. 3, pp. 842ff.

[166] See Mt. 17:22-23; 24:25; and Jn. 13:18-19.

The significance of these phrases should not be overlooked. Everything Christ did during His mission was vitally linked to heaven (Jn. 8:42). Christ's testimony about His life thoroughly incorporated the directions of His heavenly Father.

To refuse Christ's testimony is to make God out to be a liar (1 Jn. 5:7-12) and provoke a verdict of condemnation (Jn. 3:18-19, 36). In contrast, the "man who has accepted it has certified that God is truthful" (Jn. 3:34). Obviously, then, the gospel message largely makes up the testimony of Christ,[167] which originates from heaven,[168] and is itself called a "witness" (Mt. 24:14; 1 Jn. 5:10-12).

Truthfulness is an absolute necessity for a legal witness, especially for the court of heaven.[169] Thus, the Apostle John used a forensic title to describe Christ: *The Faithful and True Witness* (Rev. 3:14; cf. 1:5; 19:11).[170] Here John encompassed both the ideas of truth telling and the need for faithfulness against the pressure to compromise. Indeed, Christ's mission consisted of bearing witness to the truth (Jn. 18:37),[171] and He remained faithful to that mission even to the point of death.

The Apostles as Witnesses

In turn, Christ's life and ministry, especially His miracles, became the finger-of-God inscribed testimony on the hearts of humankind,[172] thus ensuring the veracity of His claims. Those who received His testimony also recognized its inherent commissioning as witness-followers. The very fact that Christ is a faithful witness in the courtroom of heaven, where the Father-Judge has committed all judgment to the Son, means that we, as His representative Body on earth, carry on as witnesses of the truth.[173] The Hebrew "shaliach" principle, which states that the one sent is as the one who sent him, further supports this idea.[174] Just as the Father sent the Son as an empowered witness, so the Son now sends us as similarly empowered witnesses (Jn. 5:19-30; 13:20; Jn. 20:21).

The concept of earthly mission connected to the courtroom ministry of heaven permeates Luke's record of the Acts of the Apostles. Luke combines the concrete evidence of eyewitness accounts, the testimony of Old Testament scripture (Acts 2:17-21; 25-29; 7:2ff; 13:16ff; 17:2; 28:23), and many "convincing proofs" (Acts 1:3; 3:16; 4:33; 13:9-12; 14:3; 19:11)—primarily of the Holy Spirit—to substantiate the testimony of Christ.

---

[167] See especially 1 Cor. 1:6; 2:1; 1 Tim. 2:6; 2 Tim. 1:8; 2 Thess. 1:10; and 1 Jn. 5:11-12.
[168] Mt. 13:35; Jn. 3:31-34; Eph. 1:4; 1 Pt. 1:20ff; Rev. 13:8; 17:8.
[169] For this same reason, Christ calls the Holy Spirit the "Spirit of Truth" (Jn. 14:15-18; 15:26-27; 16:12-15). As the prosecuting Advocate for the Divine Court against the world, the Holy Spirit's testimony contains absolute, accurate, convicting truth (Jn. 16:8-9).
[170] ὁ μάρτυς ὁ πιστός καί ἀληθινός. John's title for Christ echoes its antecedent pronounced to Jeremiah by the remnant of Judah: "May the LORD be a true and faithful witness against us if we do not act in accordance with everything the LORD your God sends you to tell us" (Jer. 42:5). The LXX (Jer. 49:5) has μάρτυρα δίκαιον καί πιστόν. Here the adjectives appear in reverse order, with "righteous" (δίκαιον, LXX) replacing "true" (ἀληθινός).
[171] See Mt. 10:32-33; Lk. 12:8-9; Jn. 12:27.
[172] Lk. 11:20; cf. Jn. 5:36; 10:37-38; 14:11.
[173] Note the repeated testimony about Christ by His disciples: Lk. 10:22; Jn. 21:24-25; Eph. 1:19b-22; Col. 1:15-20; He. 1:1-3; 1 Jn. 1:1-6; etc.
[174] See F. Gavin, "Shaliach and Apostolos," *ATR* 9 (1927) 250–59 and George Beasley-Murray, *Gospel of Life* (Peabody: Hendrickson Publishers, 1991) 20-21. Also see the Johannine Christology section under "Christianity and Judaism: Parting of Ways" in Ralph Martin and Peter Davids, editors, *Dictionary of the Later New Testament and It's Development* (Downers Grove: InterVarsity Press, 1997).

This represents more than simple evangelism, for Luke couches the apostolic mission in the terminology of the courtroom. For instance, the disciples were "witnesses of everything he did" (Acts 10:39; cf. 10:41; 13:30; 18:5), "all the prophets testify about him" (Acts 10:43), and the Holy Spirit is a joint witness: "We are witnesses of these things, and *so is the Holy Spirit*, whom God has given to those who obey him" (Acts 5:32). As court advocate, the Holy Spirit adds His convicting power to the testimony of the disciples (Acts 2:37) to bring about conversion.

Being witnesses of the resurrection is the clarion mission of the disciples (Acts 1:8, 22; 2:31-32; 3:15; 13:30, 37; 17:3). Paul was personally charged by the Lord to "be a witness to all men of what you have seen and heard" (Acts 22:15; cf. 23:11; 26:16), a charge that was summarized by Paul himself in Acts 20:24 and 26:16.

The disciples' message often contained language of the court. For example, Jesus "is the one whom God appointed as judge of the living and the dead" (Acts 10:42) and Paul "discoursed on righteousness, self-control and the judgment to come" (Acts 24:25). Indeed, the cosmic trial is never far from Paul's thoughts:

For he has set a day when he will judge the world with justice by the man he has appointed. He has given proof of this to all men by raising him from the dead.—Acts 17:31 (cf. 1 Cor. 15:20f)

Witness in Revelation

Unfortunately, the ears of the Laodiceans must have been especially dull to hear Christ's witness, for it was to them that Christ revealed His title as Faithful and True Witness (Rev. 3:14; cf. 20, 22). Their materialistic lukewarmness placed them in danger of violent rejection from our Lord. Contrary to their self-satisfied opinion, Christ's accurate and piercing testimony cut through their deception and exposed their pride.

The letter to the Laodiceans is one of seven "legal briefs" evaluating the condition of each church in Asia Minor measured against some aspect of the Person of Christ. In each case He "knows their deeds"—He has walked up and down among the representative church candlesticks and viewed the brightness of each church's flame of witness.[175] Thus, each letter embodies Christ's specific, faithful and true testimony.

Christ's standard of faithfulness to death became the standard for believers in these struggling churches. Christ warned the Smyrnans of coming persecution and admonished them to, "Be faithful, even to the point of death" (Rev. 2:10). Christ called Antipas "my faithful witness"[176] because he refused to renounce Christ and was subsequently put to death (Rev. 2:13). In addition, Christ's repeated appeal to overcome contains the idea of faithful witness in the face of persecution and trial.[177] Thus, Revelation demonstrates the challenge of overcoming by our testimony and a willingness to "not love (our) lives so much as to shrink from death" (Rev. 12:11).

---

[175] See Mt. 5:15; Jn. 5:35.
[176] ὁ μάρτυς μου ὁ πιστός μου (the attributive adjective construction).
[177] Rev. 2:7, 11, 17, 26; 3:5, 12, 21.

Becoming Faithful Witnesses

Christ continues His witness through us via the agency of the Holy Spirit. The Holy Spirit prosecutes the case for Christ against the world. In other words, as we share the gospel testimony, the Holy Spirit guides us and, in fact, personally testifies through us (1 Jn. 5:6; cf. Mt. 10:16-20).[178]

All believers, including New Testament prophets, receive directly from the heavenly intercessory ministry of Christ via the presence of the Council Advocate—or Holy Spirit—within us. In addition, we all have access to heaven's resources (including the Divine Council) through our connection to Christ, who is the Head of the Body and our advocate in heaven.[179]

Christ's example, as well as the example of prophets and early believers, sets the standard for faithful witnessing today. Their model leads us to:

1. Witness aware of our place in the courtroom ministry of heaven. We are connected to Christ's current ministry of advocacy and we play an important role in the cosmic trial of humankind. (Witnessing is far more than the popular notion of just sharing our testimony.)

2. Witness empowered by our present court Advocate, the Holy Spirit, who shares with us of Christ's current ministry. In this regard, both spiritual gifts and supernatural signs should follow our witness.[180]

3. Witness realizing that this is our primary calling and must be maintained against all external pressures. This determination *is* how we overcome in the face of compromise or persecution. Further, we must hold true to our witness knowing that materialism can greatly reduce our effectiveness.

4. Witness with acts of truth that bring a preserving salt against the decay brought on by falsehood in our culture. Christ's example speaks volumes against the tide of opinion accepting falsehood today. Should not the witness of the Church do the same?

---

[1] Gary M. Burge, *Interpreting the Gospel of John* (Grand Rapids: Baker Book House, 1992), 69. Quoted from C.H. Dodd, *The Interpretation of the Fourth Gospel* (Cambridge, England: Cambridge University Press, 1953), 383.
[2] Burge, 177.

---

[178] The Holy Spirit convicts "the world of guilt in regard to sin and righteousness and judgment" (Jn. 16:8). To "convict" (ἐλέγξει) is to prove legally guilty. This word may include all three legal aspects of making God's case: to investigate, expose, and convict (cf. Jn. 8:46).
[179] Eph. 1:22-23; Col. 1:18; He. 4:16; 7:24; 8:1-2; 1 Jn. 2:1.
[180] An example of this supernatural connection occurs in Matthew 10:19-20 (cf., Mk. 13:11). If unbelievers unjustly prosecute Christians before their courts (which supposedly represent God, cf. Ps. 82), the Holy Spirit will immediately prompt the Christians with what to say. This strongly suggests that the Holy Spirit supernaturally communicates with us as we represent Christ as witnesses to this world. In this regard, *I believe the gifts of the Spirit are the tools through which the will of heaven's court reaches earth.* Christ specifically tied prophecy to the advocacy ministry of the Holy Spirit in John 16:7, 13.

www.ingramcontent.com/pod-product-compliance
Lightning Source LLC
Chambersburg PA
CBHW081735180426
43194CB00060B/2708